Michael Chapel

Why a Decorated Veteran & Former Police Officer Remains
in Prison Decades After a Crime He Did not Commit

Henry Ball
with Deborah Ann Dahlmann

Michael Chapel

Why a Decorated Veteran & Former Police Officer Remains
in Prison Decades After a Crime He Did not Commit

Henry Ball
with Deborah Ann Dahlmann

ISBN:978-1-7357480-1-6 (Hardback)
ISBN:978-1-7357480-3-0 (Paperback)
ISBN:978-1-7357480-5-4 (E Book)

Acknowledgments

To April and Griffin, my heart, I love you.

Special thanks to:

Deborah Ann Dahlmann, Editor-in-Chief and my writing partner,

Jonathan Ellis, my business partner of more than twenty years,

and Steve Manko, my friend and mentor.

Philip & Tammy Owens, who believed in me and this book,
and to all the members of the Michael Chapel is Innocent Project.

Without all of you, I would not have been able to tell Michael Chapel's story.

Also, special thanks to:

Philip Sullivan, Pamela Holcombe, Ed Hanson, Boris & Robert Korczak,
and Tom Conroy. Tireless and selfless investigators who diligently sought,
uncovered, and brought the truth to light.

Cover Design by: Henry Ball

Book Design and Formatting by: Deborah Ann Dahlmann

Cover Formatting by: Todd Civin @ Civin Media Relations

Book Editing: Deborah Ann Dahlmann, Irene Ziegler, Steve Manko

'What The Witnesses Saw' Art Collection
by: Robert Davis @ Davis Advertising, Inc.

This book is dedicated to Michael and Eren.
What God has brought together,
let no man put asunder.

July 12, 1981 to Eternity

In honor of the memory of Harold and Marilyn Chapel, Michael's parents.
Both relentless believers in their son's innocence. Since Michael's arrest,
Harold spent his remaining years collecting and cataloging evidence and
documentation related to the case. His diligence and belief in his son
delivered valuable contributions to this team.

In honor of the memory of Nancy Jane West and Iva Adeline 'Pom-Pom' Blis-
sitt, Eren's mother and grandmother. Both women of strong character and
strength remained steadfast in their belief in Michael's innocence.

Michael Chapel is based on actual events. Some of the conversations are abbreviated, and others are dramatized for publication. Where direct quotes were obtained from transcripts, court documents, or other public records, it will be noted; otherwise, the dialogue may be based on interpretation of the facts on record, a preponderance of the evidence, or interviews conducted. None of the names or adjudicated events have been changed or made up, and no attempt has been made to protect any persons, parties, or organizations from the truth. Hours of interviews, research, and investigative examination have been conducted. Every effort has been made to corroborate the facts of this case. It is the hope of the publishers that this book will shine a light on the events that have kept the truth cloaked in darkness for decades.

Fiat Justitia ruat Caelum.
Let the truth prevail though the heavens fall.

Italicized conversations included in this book are taken directly from recorded events, police records, or trail transcripts.

Prelude

In August 1995, during the frenzied coverage of the O. J. Simpson trial, another highly publicized case played out in the national media: The *State of Georgia vs. Michael Harold Chapel pursuant to the 1993 robbery and murder of fifty-three-year-old Emogene Thompson.*

Described as arrogant and unrepentant by the local and national press, Chapel was tried and convicted in the highly charged court of public opinion long before he ever stepped a cowboy boot into a court of law. He sought what is promised to every American – JUSTICE.

In both courts, the lead prosecutor, Gwinnett County District Attorney Danny Porter presented a predominantly circumstantial case void of significant or demonstrable evidence. Decades later, new evidence suggests that Porter illegally withheld crucial exculpatory evidence from the defense team -- evidence that may have proven Officer Chapel innocent of the crime.

Porter steadfastly upholds Officer Chapel's prosecution and conviction. During an exit interview aired on Atlanta's *WSB Radio* following his 2020 defeat in the Gwinnett County District Attorney's race, Porter described the Chapel case as one that best defined his tenure as chief prosecutor.

There may be no doubt that this case defined Porter's career because Porter wallowed in the wrong kind of notoriety apart from it. As the District Attorney, Porter was sued for libel and slander by his successor and faced charges of misappropriation of county funds by the county's Solicitor General. Often accused of overzealous prosecution and considered a publicity hound by many, Porter contemplated switching political parties to hold on to power. A sitting district court judge accused him of computer hacking.

By his own admission, Porter is best defined as the man who refused a decorated veteran and former police officer a fair day in court. Why is Porter quoted on the *Gwinnett Daily Post*'s front page as saying, *"I would also like to find out who it is that really killed Emogene Thompson."* This telling statement was published January 1, 1997, nearly two years after convicting Michael Chapel for that very crime.

Why does Danny Porter continue to oppose Michael Chapel's parole and remain steadfast in the conviction of this man who could not have committed this heinous crime? Why does Danny Porter, as the Gwinnett County District Attorney, stand in the way of justice? Why does Michael Chapel, a devoted husband and father, a decorated veteran, and former model police officer remain in prison decades after a crime he did not commit?

In order to best answer these questions, let's go back to the roaring '90s of Metropolitan Atlanta and Georgia's Gwinnett County, a region bursting with excitement, growth, and crime.

The following events are true.

Prologue

Fifty-year-old Henry Lamar Jeffcoat pulled his pretty black Cadillac into the garage he had just opened via remote control. He looked in the rear view mirror. He saw shadowy figures moving rapidly toward him.

The two men wearing tactical gear had laid-in-wait for Jeffcoat behind the corner of his privacy fence. Jeffcoat's modest split-level home, located at the bottom of the hill on Pleasant Valley Drive in Morrow, Georgia, was an unassuming fortress. Jeffcoat was instantly ready for the two men emerging from the wooded thicket banking Panther Creek.

Jeffcoat, the popular and profitable Goldrush Show Bar owner, still carried large sums of money, even though he had been attacked two years earlier in 1991. Bandits wearing tactical gear hit him over the head with a blunt instrument, dragged him into his home, and forced him to open both safes -- the locations somehow known to the assailants. The bandits made off with over $62,000 cash and made Jeffcoat a favored target.

After the 1991 attack, Jeffcoat invested in several security measures that he now employed as the two would-be bandits slid under the rapidly closing garage door. Henry hit the car's panic button, immediately notifying Clayton County Police Department. The garage door, now sealed shut, would not open again without a disabling code.

Jeffcoat's right hand slid over the cold steel of his final security measure, a Glock 9MM semi-automatic pistol that he pulled from the center console. After a belly flop entry into the garage on the driver's side of the Cadi, off-duty Riverdale SWAT Officer Mark Douglas McKenna stood up. He started to raise the .38 revolver in his left hand when Jeffcoat opened fire.

McKenna immediately took a shot to the face that entered under his chin and exited behind the left ear, dropping him back to his belly and disabling him for the gun battle that ensued. Another Riverdale SWAT officer and McKenna's partner in the crime, James 'Jim Bob' Batsel, was quick to his feet and began to unload the fifteen-round clip of his 9MM service weapon. The shots hit Jeffcoat in the back as he turned toward Batsel, who had entered the garage on the passenger side of the Cadillac.

McKenna wailed in pain and lamentations as Jeffcoat and Batsel both emptied their carry clips, filling the garage with hot lead, thick gun

I

smoke, and the metallic smell of flowing blood. They reloaded. Jeffcoat sustained nine gunshot wounds to the back and perished during the barrage.

Saved by a department-issued bulletproof vest, Batsel realized his victim was dead. He ran to McKenna's aid. McKenna tried to get to his feet beside the vehicle, but he was bleeding, disoriented, and in great pain. Batsel attempted to open the garage only to realize he was trapped. Knowing the police would not be far away following the O. K. Corral style shootout that had just occurred, Batsel panicked. He kicked a panel on the garage door, eventually creating an escape hatch in the sealed door. He so badly damaged the door and its frame that entire structure would need to be removed and replaced.

Batsel helped McKenna through the hole and carried him through the woods that the two men had emerged from just a few minutes earlier. Batsel carried the three-hundred-pound man, wounded and flailing, down the banks of Panther Creek, across the flowing and rocky creek bed, and back up the steep wooded hill on the other side. The blood trail led investigators to the spot where the getaway driver, Christopher Thomas Grantham, picked them up.

Having heard gunfire and police sirens screaming in the midnight air, a neighbor spotted the men as they got into a blacked-out minivan. Dubbed the 'War Wagon,' the minivan sprinted South as the first respond-ing officers turned off Lake Harbin Road and raced toward the crime scene. The War Wagon was now parallel to the northbound lanes of I-75, and within thirty seconds, joined the metro melee of the six northbound lanes of speeding traffic. They blended into the crowd, shielding them from a dozen other blue lights rushing to Jeffcoat's bullet-riddled and blood-soaked garage.

Henry Jeffcoat's security measures were not enough to save him from his military and SWAT-trained attackers. Still, they were enough to put the Clayton County Police Department and a metro area joint task force hot on their trail.

By this time, the task force had been looking into the two-year-old crime spree since January and assumed they were dealing with law enforce-ment or military-trained criminals. The task force, which added feder-

Prologue

al resources after the Jeffcoat murder, believed that police and SWAT equipment, including two-way radios and tactical gear, were used. The suspects appeared to have insider knowledge about the movements and locations of the victims and where safes were kept. Now, the task force knew what the get-away vehicle looked like, and a BOLO (*be on the lookout*) went out for the blacked-out mini-van.

During the crime spree, the theft ring was responsible for some twenty known robberies or attempted robberies. These included a Home Depot store, a Wal-Mart, several other businesses, a handful of nightclubs and strip joints, a 450 lb. safe toted away like a sack of potatoes, and the previous follow-home attack on Henry Jeffcoat.

South metro business owners, particularly nightclub owners and managers, became paranoid. They increased private security, as the seemingly endless stream of brazen robberies turned deadly.

The Georgia Legislature debated the Zell Miller *'Life Without Parole'* bill aimed at stiffening penalties for violent offenders. Legislators from across the region were hungry for law enforcement to bring the lawlessness to an end.

In the days following the February 10 murder, Mark McKenna abruptly called in sick and failed to show up for duty. His partners in crime did their best to nurse the injured rogue with drugstore first aid and over-the-counter pain medicine. McKenna needed medical attention in the worst way, and he was facing the cold reality that his law enforcement career was over. There was no way he could conceal his injuries from the department, nor could he seek medical attention at a hospital, which was where he needed to be.

Seven days after the attack, Batsel reported that his SWAT gear and firearm were stolen. In a report to a fellow officer, he claimed that both were removed from his vehicle within the last two weeks, unbeknownst to him. Investigators became suspicious of Batsel and his abruptly vacationing cohort, Mark McKenna.

While Batsel was away on his track-covering mission, McKenna reached the end of his rope and reached for the phone. He called the Clayton County Police Department blowing the whistle on the whole crime ring.

McKenna was willing to cooperate in exchange for medical attention and taking the death penalty off the table.

The story and the investigation blew up in the metro area like a streaking super nova. Before anyone in the Atlanta area knew where the sleepy Texas town of Waco was located, 'roid-rage' was added to the peach state's vernacular.

The criminal cops, who ironically referred to themselves as the WBAC (*White Boys Against Crime*), were from three different metro police departments: Riverdale, Fulton County Sheriff, and Atlanta. Most of the syndicate's civilian accomplices were gym rats at a Gold's Gym in Fayetteville, Georgia. Apparently, they all abused anabolic steroids, amphetamine, and other growth and performance-enhancing drugs that led the now infamous Jim Bob Batsel to describe himself as a 'monster' following his arrest.

Local law enforcement leaders were incensed and determined to root out all the monster, roid-raging cops they could find. The task force looked back at every commercial burglary or tactical-style crime in the metro area that occurred over the last two years.

Instantly, all five cops became infamous. Details about their service records, military and job history, and social and secular activities became front-page fodder for the local press. A composite profile began to collate for the task force. Big, buff, white boys. SWAT, Military, tactical, outdoors men. Gun enthusiasts. Most of all, steroid users.

Seasonal pollen began its annual assault on middle Georgia, painting the metro area powdery yellow, while the joint task force teamed up with internal affairs agencies across the region making a list of potential WBAC and checking it twice.

A veteran cop in Gwinnett County believed to fit the profile to a tee was Michael Chapel. Leader of Gwinnett County's nationally ranked SWAT team, Chapel was the epitome of a big, buff white boy, standing nearly 6'7" tall, weighing in at roughly 290 pounds of lean muscle mass. He was an avid archer and outdoors man and a small health and fitness gym owner where he and several fellow officers' weight-trained daily.

Prologue

Gwinnett County had its own rash of unsolved burglaries. These included several businesses, restaurants, and an attorney's office safe holding a large sum of cash that was burglarized.

In mid-March, a sting operation believed to be linked to the joint task force was green-lit. An Internal Affairs Investigator, Greg Browning, and another man named Yeager, claiming to be a federal agent, visited Chapel's gym. Browning and 'Special Agent' Yeager told Chapel they were seeking intel on a person of interest that might be known to Chapel—Steve Mitchell, a local rabble-rouser. They informed Chapel that Mitchell was suspected of domestic terrorism and believed he was planning a deadly attack of some sort. They did not have enough for a warrant, but wanted Chapel to see if he could help track Mitchell.

Chapel knew of Mitchell but had not seen him recently. Mitchell had owned an auto parts store, Street Magic, on Moreno Street, not far from the current location of Chapel's Iron World Gym. Mitchell allegedly blamed Gwinnett County Police Department's Captain Cantrell for destroying his business in the late '80s and constantly told local business-people, including Chapel, that *they* were out to get him.

Chapel related to Browning and Yeager that Mitchell claimed to be a Vietnam Marine veteran, a mercenary, and had mentioned to Chapel once that he lived in the woods behind his Hall County residence because *they* would not find him there. Admittedly, Chapel always dismissed Mitchell as a nut case and Hall County's problem. According to Special Agent Yeager, he might be everybody's problem.

After having received the BOLO for Mitchell, Chapel wondered how dangerous Mitchell might be. He never thought of him as much of a danger; and he never considered that Mitchell was being used as part of a ruse to flush out roid-raging cops.

On April 8, 1993, one week before anyone outside of Buford, Georgia and Gwinnett County had ever heard of Michael Chapel, Steve Mitchell—outfitted in camouflaged fatigues, tactical boots, black Ray-Bans, and carrying a small green, military-style duffel bag—walked into Iron World gym.

"Big Mike!" Mitchell bellowed into the gym, summoning Chapel to the front.

"Be right with you, sir," Chapel said. He was weight-training a regular client. Recognizing Mitchell and thinking he might have a prime opportunity to help Investigator Browning, Chapel motioned to a gym assistant, Casandra Rice, to take over his personal training session. He told her to be alert as he might need her help.

Chapel approached Mitchell with a welcoming demeanor. "Hey, Steve. What's going on, sir?"

"Can we talk in private?"

"Yeah, come on into my office."

Chapel led Mitchell into his small office. He had a window that allowed him to monitor the PT in progress, so he opened the shade and said, "Gotta keep an eye on this PT. Don't want my clients getting hurt."

"No doubt, Jar-head," Mitchell said stepping towards Chapel's desk. "I got something to show you." Mitchell opened the taut end of the duffel and poured its contents onto Chapel's desk.

"That's a lot of cash, Mitchell," Chapel said, surprised to see over $20,000 in banded Benjamins piled on top of his loose paperwork. "Where'd you come across that much cash?"

"Some jobs, nothing too far outside the law," Mitchell boasted, then set the trap. "You want in, Big Mike?"

Chapel was skeptical, but played along, "Steve, what are we talking about here, and what do you mean not too far outside the law?"

"Well, nothing you'd go to prison for, I don't think, but you might not want to tell that son-of-a-bitch, Cantrell, about it." Mitchell continued being vague. Mike looked out the viewing window and made an excuse to step out.

"Hold on a second, Steve," Chapel said, "this girl is going to hurt my client."

Prologue

"No, no, not like that!" He went over to the weight press and demonstrated a proper squatting technique. With his back turned to the view window, Chapel dropped a business card and told Cassandra Rice to call the number on the back of the card and ask for Greg Browning.

"Tell him Steve Mitchell is in my office with a bag full of cash talking about some unlawful jobs," Mike said quietly and clearly. Rice nodded and went back to instructing the PT client while Chapel returned to his office. Once he entered the office, he positioned himself with his back to the view window, ostensibly obstructing Mitchell's view of the gym, Rice walked briskly to the breakroom and called the number for Gwinnett County Police Department Internal Affairs. Three attempts to get Browning on the phone failed, while Chapel continued his conversation with Mitchell.

"So, tell me about these jobs, Steve," Chapel persisted, "That's a lot of money for something almost legal."

"Well, you know Mike—" Mitchell did a little fishing of his own. "People are willing to pay for skills like ours."

"What skills are we talking about?"

"You know, Jar-head!" Mitchell called him by the Marine nomenclature. "Special forces type stuff. We're warriors!"

"I don't know about that, brother," Chapel said, nodding toward the money still laying on his desk. "I'm just a beat cop. Nobody paying me that kind of money."

"Well, Chappy," Mitchell said, as he crammed the cash in the duffel bag, "Maybe I can help you with that, but I gotta go for now."

"Don't be in a hurry, Steve," Chapel said, trying to prolong the visit. "Let's talk about these jobs."

"Another time, Chappy," Mitchell said as he hurried to the door.

Chapel thought about holding him until Browning arrived, but there was no warrant he was aware of, and nothing Mitchell said would rise to probable cause, so Chapel patted him on the shoulder and said, "Let me know when you're ready to talk."

After Mitchell left, Cassandra Rice rushed into Chapel's office. "I couldn't get Browning on the phone, and the lady I did talk to acted like she didn't want to talk to me!"

"That's odd," Chapel said. "Let me try."

Chapel had the same difficulty reaching Browning, but he finally got Internal Affairs Agent Monica Hack on the phone. Hack was a former beat cop and one-time shift partner to Chapel in Buford. Chapel related to Hack all the pertinent information about the interaction with Steve Mitchell. He described the money, and a receipt, which had fallen onto Chapel's desk with the cash. Mitchell claimed the receipt was for a car loan pay-off. Chapel offered to assist Internal Affairs in the investigation and asked Hack to relay the message to Browning and Yeager.

Greg Browning shook his head at his commanding officer, Lt. Mike Powell. "I don't know, boss. We set the bait, and Chapel bobbed at the hook as you'd expect from a righteous cop."

"Do you think he smelled a rat?" Powell asked.

"I don't think so, boss. He seems genuine to me. I think he was just doing his job. I mean, I know he fits the profile. Hell, he could be twins with that deputy from Fulton County, William Moclaire, but we dropped twenty-grand in his lap, and he just did his job."

"I'll brief the task force, but keep digging and let me know when something pops up."

"Will do, boss." Browning pulled the door to Powell's office closed behind him. *This is such a waste of time. This guy is clean.* Browning thought.

Springtime was in full bloom when ten-year veteran police officer Michael Chapel himself became the subject of a secret investigation. Investigators had a suspect and were in search of a crime. He had been the subject of a baited sting operation that placed $20,000 firmly in his clutches, from a man he believed to be a dangerous domestic terrorist, and his only reaction was to do his job and uphold the law.

The suspicion unknown to Chapel, but swirling around him was because he matched some aspects of a profile developed as a result of one small and isolated group of rogue cops who chose to run afoul of the law almost as soon as they decided to join the force. Most of the officers in the WBAC joined their respective forces in 1989, and by 1991 they were immersed in their clandestine crime syndicate, fueled by unhealthy and out-of-control drug addiction.

The steroids epidemic was not just an Atlanta Metro phenomenon. It was quickly becoming a national problem. In 1993 the *Atlanta Journal-Constitution* reported that massive amounts of anabolic steroids were entering the United States through the world's busiest land port, connecting San Diego with Tijuana at the US – Mexico Border.

By 2005, *ABC News* was reporting on roid-raging cops from coast to coast. There were significant scandals in New York City, Spokane, Washington, Norman, Oklahoma, and across the country. Officers abused steroids and other human growth drugs to bulk up, often at the expense of their good judgment and mental acuity. The WBAC from Atlanta was *ABC's* first example.

A police psychologist in Washington, Dr. Gene Sanders, estimated that five percent of the police force either used or had used steroids. With many of the abusers resorting to major crimes in order to fund their habits and secret lifestyles. It was not an issue that any department could take lightly.

There was another issue facing police forces across the nation. During the '90s, police profiling became a political and public hot potato.

In the mid '90s, Atlanta became the epicenter of misapplied profiles and ruined reputations as Kathy Scruggs, and other Atlanta beat reporters honed their profiling skills with the notorious WBAC. Soon, journalism devolved into speculation, innuendo, and flat-out falsehoods about 'out of control killer cop – Michael Chapel.'

In 1996, during the much-anticipated Summer Olympic Games, a bomb went off in Centennial Olympic Park. Hero-painted-villain, Richard Jewell, a Gwinnett County resident, would have his life infamously ruined by Scruggs, the *Atlanta Journal-Constitution*, and an arrogantly compartmentalized FBI that choose to prosecute a profile rather than study the facts of the case.

The FBI created a hypothetical profile of a lone bomber/wannabe cop. Suspicion fell on the security guard who discovered the bomb whose decisive actions potentially saved hundreds of lives. When the identify leaked from the FBI to the *AJC*'s Kathy Scruggs, a reporter struggling with her own addictions and ambitions, the investigation became a three-ring circus. Richard Jewell became an ignominious reminder that profiling is a dangerous and inexact science.

Michael Chapel watched it all unfold from a prison forged of the same steel.

Michael
Chapel

One

*D*riving rain poured for most of the evening. Brisk gusts of forty miles per hour, tornado-generating thunderstorms, and heavy cloud cover created limited visibility. Officer Michael Chapel strapped on his yellow rain pants in the kitchenette of the day room at Firehouse Fourteen on Buford Highway. He retrieved his service weapon from the island counter top, a Smith and Wesson Semi-Automatic .45, and holstered it.

"It's time to go check on the Van Man," Chapel announced as he prepared to make his nightly visit to the gym he owned on Moreno Street before he would wrap up his patrol for shift change at 2230 hours.

"How can you eat that junk, Rooster?" Chapel said to his supervisor, Sergeant D. E. 'Rooster' Stone, who stood at the kitchenette's dining area eating a second candy bar. "All that sugar isn't good for your system."

Stone shrugged sheepishly. Even though he was the superior officer, Chapel was the Northside Precinct's fitness guru. The rebuke forgotten when Chapel responded via shoulder mic to Detective Danny Smith from Robbery Division. Detective Smith offered more details related to a suspect known as 'Peaches.' Both he and Chapel were in hot pursuit of this suspect.

"Got the warrants signed. They're on my desk if you run across Peaches." Detective Smith's update was cut short with an assignment from Police Dispatch at 2156. It was Thursday, April 15, 1993.

Fire Station Fourteen and Northside Police Precinct shared the same building. Northside officers regularly passed through the firehouse and its day room. Snacks were plentiful, and a wide variety of drinks were always cold. The television played a movie on local broadcast as the first responders kept up with the weather tracker at the bottom of the screen.

"How can we tell when that dark red band is going to hit us?" Officer Brian Reddy asked as the men watched a local reporter describe the destructive band of thunderstorms rolling through the region.

"Do you not see the green highlighted box right here?" Chapel mocked. He pointed to the city of Buford within the bounds of that highlighted box and covered by the first shades of red.

"You patrol there every day, Buddy," Rooster added, as lightening flashed outside. Thunder rumbled as if to accentuate the point, "and it sounds pretty red out there right now."

"It's raining. I can tell you that," said Engineer Stan Wilson. "Now, let's get back to the game!" The banter returned to the debate of the Atlanta Braves' six to one loss to the San Francisco Giants. The movie playing in the background, forgotten.

Candlestick Park's day game would prove to be the opening salvo in a wire-to-wire pennant race, which *The Yearly Reader* still lists as *The Last Great Pennant Race*. As the officers debated, they took turns imitating the Braves freshly acquired pitching ace, Greg Maddux, and threw crumpled pieces of paper at each other while the hazardous storm hovered and raged outside.

The second shift officers had elected to ride out the storm together at the firehouse. They snacked and argued the finer points of their baseball expertise.

"Sttttttriiike two!" called Wilson, as Officer Brian Reddy used his baton to swing futilely at the crumpled curve offered by Firefighter David Pierce, Jr.

"Over the plate, Junior!" Reddy complained.

One

"Dude, you're no Neon Deion!" Pierce scoffed, referring to Atlanta's prime-time star, Deion Sanders, who had provided the Braves' only offense that day with a solo home run in the top of the eighth inning.

"Just sayin'," Reddy continued. "Gimme something I can hit!"

"We don't have the broad side of a barn in here, Officer Mendoza, just a day room," Firefighter Bob Sloan cracked, and laughter erupted.

Standing inside the building, Chapel knew dispatch could hear the rumblings of the fire station, including its constantly squawking radio scanner with the loudspeaker directly over his right shoulder. He had been here before, and it did not seem to cause much distraction. Both he, Reddy, and their immediate supervisor, Sergeant Stone, were at the fire station regularly.

"Come on, Chapel," Pierce chided as the paper ball sliced the right side of Chapel's upper arm. "Some kind of outfielder you are!"

"Ten-seven-six," Chapel said and gave the en-route code to dispatch, ignoring the firehouse's resident comedian.

"Gotta go. Domestic. Duty calls." He nodded goodbye to the other eight men. Chapel exited the building through the small portico at the back door that provided a little shelter for the firemen's bar-b-que grill and the ashtray used by the few who still smoked cigarettes.

Officer Chapel jogged thirty feet to the driver's door of his patrol car backed into a space by the retaining wall next to Stone's vehicle. Stone's also drove a 1993 Crown Victoria Police Interceptor, white with a reflective blue stripe and department identified. Chapel climbed into the driver's seat, reached into his Pro-Gard Police Pursuit Pack, and retrieved a small washcloth. He attempted to dry his hair and forehead drenched from the short jog to the car. *'I need to find that damn head-cover!'* He thought aloud and pulled the column gear shifter into drive exiting the parking lot. Destination: Arden Drive. Domestic disturbance, kids fighting, a routine 10-16.

Chapel made a brief stop at his gym, Iron World, located six minutes from the precinct. He collected the maroon leather zip-up People's Bank and Trust bag, holding the day's receipts prepared by trusted gym member and part-time manager, Van Parker. He checked his office for the missing black trooper-style head-cover. Bingo. He spoke briefly to Dana Blount and other patrons working out. He always made a point of being visible and available in his determination to build lasting relationships.

"Thanks, Van Man. Keep up the good work."

He arrived at the scene of the domestic disturbance approximately thirteen minutes after the dispatch call.

Roughly four minutes after Chapel received the dispatch call, at approximately 2200, residents at the northern end of Gwinnett County heard two successive loud bangs ring out through the stormy night.

"Everything okay back there?" Jane Bagley asked her husband as he re-entered their log cabin-style home on Hill Crest Drive. Gwinnett County Fire Department Engineer Terry Bagley had gone outside to retrieve his uniform from the laundry room built onto their back porch. Terry and Jane were preparing for bed, as Terry was to be the Acting Officer for A Shift at Firehouse Fourteen the next morning.

"I think somebody just got shot-shot," Bagley said, responding to his wife.

"That's not funny, T-Bags!" Jane shot back and headed to the bedroom.

The Bagley's climbed into bed, as Emogene Thompson lay dead in front of the Gwinnco Muffler Shop off Peachtree Industrial Boulevard, near Georgia Highway 20 in Sugar Hill. The driving rain poured through the partially opened driver's window of her 1986 brown and tan Lincoln Continental. Left in the locked vehicle, with a flat tire, shot twice, her body slumped over the center console with her seatbelt loosely fastened. It was tucked under the left arm instead of over the left shoulder. Her settling blood drained from two bullet wounds in her head soaking through the driver's seat and pooling on the floorboard behind the passenger front seat rest.

Fireman Craig Ellington, stationed at Gwinnett Fire House One in

One

Norcross, made coffee for the A Shift crew arriving for duty. He heard the call over the scanner for a possible two-eleven, one-eighty-seven – robbery, homicide – with the deceased person on location. It was Friday morning, just after 0800.

Hours after the shift was in full swing, Ellington stared at the crime scene broadcast on the station's day room television. He watched the victim's car being loaded onto a flatbed tow truck under the watchful eye of Gwinnett County Police Officer Ed Byers.

Ellington mused out loud, "Dumb criminals." He fixed his attention on the flat tire, "Must be an attempt to cover their tracks. Vic had to know the killer." Ellington surmised that if the victim had pulled over for a flat tire, 'a good Samaritan bandit' had no way of knowing that the woman inside the distressed vehicle carried a large amount of cash, as announced by an on-scene reporter.

Responding Officer Ed Byers noted in his report filed later that day: "While the victim's vehicle was pulled onto a Brown and Brown rollback wrecker, this officer observed two cuts on the sidewall of the flat tire."

Crime scene investigators were about twenty hours into a separate homicide on the South end of Peachtree Industrial Boulevard in Norcross. A Korean store owner was murdered when her husband went for lunch on the 15th of April. Exhausted investigators arrived on the scene at the Thompson murder at the North end of Peachtree Industrial Boulevard at 0853 on April 16 and worked through the day combing the vehicle and its location—the Gwinnco Muffler property.

The collected evidence included one empty white envelope bearing the name of the victim's son – Michael (Thompson). Included was a lid and straw from a Subway drink cup, a Styrofoam cup, a pair of broken eyeglasses, a beige umbrella, a cigarette case and lighter, a box of tissue, and a loose tissue. There was a couple of receipts, a miscellaneous piece of white paper, ten dollars cash, and several loose coins in the cigarette case. Resting in plain sight on the passenger-side dashboard was a long-stemmed yellow rose still in its cellophane packaging indicative of that used by floral retailers. Also found, the first of two .38 caliber slugs, the second found during a subsequent search.

Michael Chapel

A crime scene technician snapped photos of minimal blood spatter inside the car, a pool of blood on the driver's seat, and behind the passenger seat, streams of blood that ran up the back of the victim's neck, and blood droplets on the rubber seal of the closed and locked passenger door. There were more blood droplets outside the vehicle on both sides of the car.

The vehicle was dusted for latent fingerprints. Other than those of the victim, there was a set of prints on the vehicle's passenger-side dashboard. These fingerprints belonged to an unidentified person described by ID technicians as 'small for an adult.'

Michael Thompson arrived on the scene at 0853, virtually the same time as the CSI team arrived. "That's my mother in that car!" he called out as Officer Ed Byers held him thirty-five feet behind his mother's automobile.

"Are you sure that's your mother, sir?" Detective Tony Ervin asked, walking towards the young man and Officer Byers.

"Well, um, it's her car, right?" Thompson back-peddled.

"I don't know, sir. What's your mother's name?" Ervin asked, then added, "And, uh, do you mind if I ask to see your ID, Mr. uh? What's your full name?"

"Uh, well, um, Michael Keith Thompson." The scrawny, fidgety young man reached into his back pocket to retrieve his wallet. "Have you found her purse?" he asked.

"I'm not sure if a purse was retrieved or not, Mr. Thompson." Ervin returned Thompson's ID. "Should we be looking for it for any particular reason?" Ervin sensed the young man was more interested in confirming the location of his mother's pocketbook than confirming that the deceased was, in fact, his mother or the person in the vehicle was, in fact, deceased.

"Well, um, she had about $7,000 in cash in that purse," Thompson said, and instantly GCPD knew that this was no happenstance meeting to fix a flat tire. The victim's purse, described as a crème-colored leather bag, was nowhere to be found. In addition, no cash was found in the vehicle other than that listed on the evidence list – approximately $11.

The District Attorney's investigation, running parallel to Gwinnett County Police Department's Investigation, would initially focus on Michael Thompson and a known associate, Dennis Shelton. During this phase of the investigations, it was learned that in addition to a crack cocaine addiction, Thompson was a frequent flyer at a local pay-by-the-hour motel. There, prostitution of both the hetero and homosexual variety was reportedly the leading commerce, followed closely by the illicit drug trade and illegal gaming.

During questioning, Thompson claimed that he had dinner with his mother at the Waffle House across the street from the Police Precinct on the night of the murder. Thompson told Detective Ervin that he last saw his mother at 8:00 pm. A few days later, he told Burnette that he last saw her at 8:30 pm.

He claimed he left to watch TV with friends while his mother went to work. He returned home after 10:00 pm. Emogene had already left for work. Thompson said he watched a horror movie until he went to bed at 11:30 pm. He denied making any phone calls or speaking to anyone else during this time. Phone records show a call made to a drug dealer in Hiawassee, Georgia, shortly before 11:00 pm.

Next door neighbor, Amy Parker claimed that Michael Thompson had been at her home all day and left sometime between 8:00 and 9:30 pm to go to Subway. He returned about an hour later with a Subway drink cup and brownies. After watching a few minutes of *The Simpsons*, Thompson left to '*see about a job*' and returned about 10:30 pm. Parker said Thompson finally went home around 11:00 pm. However, she did not *hear* him leave again. She also indicated that she and her boyfriend looked up at 9:50 pm to see Emogene Thompson leave for work at her regular time.

Amy Parker's boyfriend, Keith Seay, gave a third version of events. He claims that Amy Parker left their trailer after 9:30 pm to use the phone at the nearby Thompson home. When he looked out the window, noting that Emogene Thompson's driveway was not visible while seated on the couch, he said he saw Amy Parker walking with and talking to Ms. Thompson as she got into her car at around 9:50 pm.

Michael Chapel

According to Keith Seay's father, Wheldon Seay, Amy Parker told him that she had gone over to use the phone. This revelation makes Amy Parker the last person, other than the killer or killers, to see her alive.

Michael Thompson did not provide a corroborated alibi and would have been one of the last two people to see his mother alive. However, he also told police that Dennis Shelton was present on at least one occasion when his mother's money, stashed behind a makeshift armoire in their living room, went missing.

In front of Wheldon Seay, Amy bragged (something she later called a joke) that she and her baby daddy, Dwayne 'Scooter' Coggins, could easily slip into Emogene Thompson's trailer and take her money. This interaction happened days before the initial $7,000 burglary. Scooter Coggins was known to GCPD. He had killed a man when he was fourteen years old, though never charged. Jack Burnette allegedly called it 'a needed killing,' due to the extensive criminal record of the victim, Douglas Leon Coggins. Ironically, Chapel received a letter of commendation dated April 15, 1992, from the department for solving that case.

Dennis Shelton was also known to investigators, including Detective Erving. Shelton was believed to have been involved in a homicide that transpired in Sugar Hill within the last year. A then unidentified Russian was found dead near the Craig Road area. Detective Ervin had sent Chapel to rattle Shelton's cage, and he did just that during a civilian ridealong a week before Chapel's first contact with Emogene Thompson.

Soon after, Ervin and Detective L. Hinton questioned Shelton about the robbery and murder of Emogene Thompson. Her body had been discovered less than twelve hours earlier. When asked for his whereabouts on the night in question, Shelton said he was with his girlfriend, Cynthia 'Chari' King. When questioned, King gave a different answer. They had been together earlier in the evening, she said but parted company sometime before the medical examiner's window of death.

Shelton had no alibi, and when asked about his relationship with Thompson, he told Ervin and Hinton that he stopped hanging around with Thompson when he saw him kissing a man. This denial of friendship became more curious when it was learned that Shelton's father,

8

Richard Shelton, posted bond for Thompson when District Attorney
Danny Porter was secretly prosecuting him before Chapel's trial.

Another neighbor, Marsha Smith, told investigators that her daughter
had dated Dennis Shelton, and Shelton involved her daughter in drugs
and a burglary that Michael Chapel solved. Chapel also helped the girl
get into rehab, where she remained for treatment. Smith told District
Attorney Senior Investigator Dave Baker that Michael Thompson had located his mother's hiding place for the stashed $14,000 and showed it to
Dennis Shelton. A couple of days later, half of the money was stolen. She
related that she was personally scared of Shelton, and she maintained
that Shelton was the murderer.

"I like this kid Shelton for murder, sir," Dave Baker said to Gwinnett
County's top prosecutor, District Attorney Danny Porter. "He lied to us
about his whereabouts. He lied about his connections with the victim's
son. The latent fingerprints on the dash are consistent with his print size.
Once the lab is through with their analysis, I'm almost certain we can tie
him to the scene."

"Don't we believe the shots came from the back seat?" DA Porter said.
"And what about the witnesses who claimed he saw a cop at the scene?"

"Maybe he did see a cop. It was dark, but that old yellow striped squad
car is hard to miss, even in limited visibility," Baker said. "I feel certain
the perp had at least one accomplice. The shots could've come from the
backseat or someone outside the vehicle if the vic's head was turned
toward the passenger side and downward. Either way, there was at
least one passenger in the car. Think about it. How else would the
blood droplets land in the passenger door jamb and outside the vehicle,
especially considering the fact that all the doors were found closed and
locked."

Porter tossed the crime scene photos aside. "That could also explain the
limited blood spatter?"

"It could, maybe. A passenger or passengers would have absorbed
some of the spatter. And since there is a bullet hole in the middle of the
passenger seat, the passenger either got out of the vehicle just before the
shots were fired or got out between shots because the second shot was

point-blank to the back of the victim's already slumped head."

"Ergo, some spatter, but not as much as you would expect in the front and upper part of the car, but plenty of blood in the driver's seat, directly under the vic's slumped head, and on the floorboard in the back seat," Porter said. He liked what they were piecing together.

"Exactly!" Baker replied.

"Okay," Porter said. "We can establish multiple perps, but do we have enough on Shelton to place him in the car? And" he continued, "who was the cop? Was he the trigger? And what's his tie to Shelton?"

"That's a little trickier, sir," Baker said. "The only boxy white patrol car the department has with a yellow stripe is the spare. It is not assigned to anyone at the moment. So, every cop at the precinct could have had access to it, and the description of the alleged cop could fit about ninety percent of the officers on the force."

"Have we run forensics on the spare car?" Porter asked, his patience waning.

"We're working on that, sir. I've asked PD to secure the car, but so far, I haven't received a response." Baker leaned in. "I believe Shelton is the weak link in this, sir. If we arrest him and threaten to prosecute him as an adult, he'll break and give us his accomplices, including the cop."

Porter nodded. "Makes sense, Dave. Take Tracey Barnhart and canvas that neighborhood one more time. See if you can come up with anything else on Shelton or the son, and let's prepare the affidavit. We need to get it to a judge ASAP. We can close this one quick, a big win for everybody." Porter grinned. Solving a murder case quickly would bring coveted media attention. He could hardly wait.

Two

*O*fficer Chapel learned of Emogene Thompson's death and the investigation into the apparent robbery and murder on Friday morning, April 16, at Iron World Gym. Northside Precinct's second shift regularly began their day with a team-building workout. Officer Chapel reminded Sergeant Stone and the other second shift watch partner, Brian Reddy, that he had been at the firehouse that night and had responded to a burglary call at the Thompson residence less than two weeks ago.

"Emogene Thompson?" Officer Chapel was astounded. "That's the lady on Craig Drive who refused to press charges against her son for stealing $7,000."

"Yep," confirmed Stone, "same lady. And get this, her son showed up to the scene this morning looking for her purse."

Chapel raised an eyebrow, "I'm a little surprised he didn't already know where her purse was."

"The odd thing," Stone explained, "was that the kid seemed to know his mother was dead but never once asked how she died, even though they never let him get close enough to the car to see inside. So, I think they might be looking at him as a prime suspect."

"I wouldn't have made him for a killer." Chapel said. "He's too fidgety and nervous, but that crowd he runs with, pretty dangerous bunch. I wouldn't put anything past 'em."

"I think they're talking to Amy Parker and a few others from that crew, too," Sergeant Stone said. "Somebody knows something. Right now, the bigger issue is a witness that places a uniform cop and patrol car at the scene around the time of death. This case is going to be watched and run from on high."

"Is the witness credible?" asked Officer Brian Reddy, astounded by the detail. "I mean, do they really think a cop was involved?"

"Too early to tell," Stone responded, "but it's got everyone's attention, and we need to find out. Oh, that reminds me, homicide wants to run a road check in front of the crime scene. See if we can find any more witnesses that might be frequent flyers down Peachtree Industrial Boulevard at that time of night. I need you both 10-8 by 2100 sharp."

"Ten-4, boss," confirmed Chapel.

"One more thing, Chapel," Stone said as his two watch officers completed their morning workout.

"Yeah?"

"Did you ever finish filling out that initial report?"

"No, sir. Sorry," Chapel said. "We took off to that next call, and I threw it in my do bag."

"Okay, no big deal," Stone assured, "but get it finished and turn it in when you get a chance."

"You got it, Rooster." Chapel said. "You know how I loooove paperwork!"

"I do." Stone smiled, then added, "I also need you to contact Burnette ASAP and debrief him on your contacts with the victim."

"Roger that." Chapel acknowledged the command.

Two

Instead of finishing the planned workout, Chapel made his way to the precinct, where Captain L. O. Cantrell's scheduled phone conference was already underway.

"You're right, Jack. We need to get to the bottom of this ASAP. We can't have police officers accused of murder. I'm just glad to know my guys are alibied. All three were at the firehouse."

"We'll be covering all the bases, Captain. Just need to hear what Chapel can give me on that burglary over there at the victim's place." Burnette replied.

According to Investigator Burnette's handwritten notes from April 16, the first day of the investigation, at 1:50 pm, Chapel provided him with the pertinent information regarding Emogene Thompson and her son, Michael.

On Saturday, April 3, 1993, before shift change from the first shift patrol-man, J. P. Morgan, to the second shift patrolman, Michael Chapel, the call center received a call from Emogene Thompson regarding a burglary at her residence. The dispatcher held the call through the shift change since the call was not deemed urgent.

Officer Chapel's first call that shift was a 4-59 – burglary – at the home of Emogene Thompson, a single-wide and not particularly well-maintained trailer located on Craig Drive in the Apple Valley Trailer Park. Apple Valley was a neighborhood of primarily moderate to well-maintained mobile homes where GCPD regularly responded to domestic disturbances, drug-related crimes, and occasionally, more serious calls.

Officer Chapel jotted down the tag number of the Lincoln in the drive-way, as was his custom, notified dispatch 10-8, walked up the drive past an old dark blue and partially rusted Buick. He continued up the rickety steps onto the deck that led to the front door. Emogene Thompson opened the door and invited him in before he could raise a hand to knock.

Officer Chapel found an anxious and distraught older woman who believed that someone had entered her home and stolen half of the cash that she had duct-taped in a large manila envelope behind a large secondhand armoire in her living room.

Chapel learned from this conversation with Ms. Thompson that she had recently received a $10,000 installment from a life insurance benefit paid upon the passing of her live-in boyfriend the previous year. Ms. Thompson said the hidden envelope contained over $14,000, all one hundred-dollar bills, at the time of the theft.

Officer Chapel learned that Ms. Thompson's twenty-five-year-old son, Michael, who sat on the couch and avoided eye contact throughout the visit, was the only other resident at the dwelling. According to Ms. Thompson, Michael had recently stolen $400 from the stash, and she believed he was the only person who knew where the money was hidden.

"Any idea where this money went, son?" Chapel asked sternly, trying to force eye contact with his prime suspect. Michael Thompson shifted, his eyes skirting, but did not respond. Chapel turned back to his mother.

"Ma'am, did you say you have reason to believe that someone broke in here?"

"I think they came in through the cut screen and broken window on the back door." She led Officer Chapel down the short hallway toward the master bedroom across from the semi-enclosed area that served as the home's laundry. Chapel looked at the window and noted that it had been broken for some time. Dust and cobwebs collected around the opening, and the screen indeed had been cut. The cut, more than likely made with a knife, was pushed outward from inside the dwelling.

"Ma'am, this doesn't look like forced entry," Chapel explained. He pointed out the conditions he observed.

"Well, that's strange," said Ms. Thompson.

Back in the living room, Chapel and Ms. Thompson found Michael nervously tapping a cigarette on his box of Marlboro 100s.

"Michael, you want to tell me what you know about all this?" Chapel asked again, this time in a more supportive tone.

Two

"I don't know nothin', man!" Thompson said. "I came home the other day, and she just started yelling at me about stealin' her money. That's all I know."

"Well, honey, you did help yourself to $400 a couple of weeks ago," Ms. Thompson stated. "You already told me you did it."

"That was just $400, and I told you I'ma pay you back as soon as I can, Mom!" he said, still tapping the cigarette like he was tapping out a Morse code message for help.

"Why don't you step outside for a minute and smoke that cigarette, son. Let me talk to your mom for a few?" Chapel said.

"Um, okay, well, yeah, I could use a smoke, but I didn't steal 'er money, man." Thompson exited the trailer and slammed the door.

Officer Chapel looked skeptically at Ms. Thompson, "He stole your money, ma'am. You know that, right?"

"Oh, I don't think my sweet Mikey would do that to his own mama. I mean $7,000? I just can't believe it!" Ms. Thompson protested.

"Well, ma'am, you did indicate that he stole from you before. You also told me that Mikey was the only other person who knew where you kept the money, which I must admit, is a pretty good hiding place. If a burglar had come into your home, we would surely have signs of forced entry from the outside. And without previous knowledge of your hiding place, he would have demolished your home before finding it." Chapel was cautious and respectful in speaking with Ms. Thompson. He sensed that she trusted easily, and he knew pushing the truth about her son would break her heart.

"What if we forgot to lock the door? Maybe they got in like that?" Officer Chapel understood why Ms. Thompson would grasp at this straw. His mother would never believe that he would steal from the family. But Ms. Thompson's son had taken money from her before. 'Mikey' was out for himself.

"Even if the door was open, no burglar is going to come in and steal half the money, ma'am. It's just not done," Chapel said.

"Oh, my, what should I do, Officer Chapel?" Ms. Thompson pleaded, "That's a lot of money, and I can't afford just to lose it!"

"I could arrest him," Chapel said. "Bring him in for questioning, try to ascertain what he did with the money. Then, maybe we can still recover some of it."

"Arrest him and take him to jail?" She seemed stunned. "Oh, heavens no! I don't want my baby goin' back to jail! Please, there must be another way?"

"Well, Ma'am," Chapel said as he considered her options. "If you don't wish to press charges, there's not much we can do. However, I would recommend putting the rest of the money in a safe deposit box at a bank or some secure place where only you have access."

Chapel motioned for Michael Thompson to come back inside, then confronted him with his suspicions. Thompson vehemently denied he was the culprit and refused to answer any other questions. Soon after, Ms. Thompson declined to press charges. There was no evidence to contradict Michael Thompson's denial or corroborate a break-in. Chapel handed Ms. Thompson his business card.

"The number to reach me during the daytime is here on the back. It's the number to my gym where I spend most days before 2:00 pm. After that, you can reach me here at the precinct." He pointed to the precinct number on the front of the card. "You may have to leave a message with dispatch, and they'll get in touch with me. Don't hesitate to call if you decide you want to move forward or get additional information that might help locate your funds."

Ms. Thompson accepted the card and thanked him.

Chapel ducked to clear the header jamb on his exit and queued his shoulder mic to dispatch. "32"– *no report requested.*

"Three sixty-one to three thirty-two, you copy?" Chapel's radio squawked.

Two

"Go ahead, Rooster, I copy."

"Meet me down at the vacant over on Hillcrest. Copy?"

"Ten-4, boss. 10-76." Chapel pulled into the vacant lot two blocks away from the Thompson's trailer. He parked next to his shift Sergeant who had backed into the lot.

"Burglary?"

"Not really. The son is a druggie, and I'm pretty sure he runs with that little Amy Parker's crew. She's the next-door neighbor."

"Just because he's a druggie doesn't mean he took the money. Any sign of forced entry?" Rooster asked, playing devil's advocate.

"No." Chapel recounted to his supervisor what he found at the back door and the fact of Michael's previous theft. "And the coup de grâce – the thief left half the money, another $7,000 in the same envelope, in the same hiding place."

"Oh, yeah. The son did it!" Rooster said. "You're writing a report?"

"None requested, boss. The vic is refusing to press."

"Might be a good idea just to CYA, Chapel," Stone said. "I know you hate unnecessary paperwork, but you might want a paper trail when the druggie gets around to stealing the rest of his mother's money."

"Good point, sir," Chapel said and pulled his report book from the pursuit pack. He barely scribbled a header when another call came from dispatch.

"Three sixty-one responding, 10-76," Sergeant Stone shot back, nodding to Chapel. His rear tires spun before gripping the pavement. Rooster was off.

"Three thirty-two, responding, 10-76," said Officer Chapel into his microphone and backed onto Hillcrest Drive. He shifted the column into drive and sped off to catch the Rooster. Simultaneously, he pulled the report off his notebook and shoved it into his do bag. He would finish the report later, he assured himself.

Hours later, dispatch called out for an aggravated domestic, "All units, we have an eighty-six agg at Power Ave. Possible male attacking female. Please respond?"

Officer Chapel responded first. "Three thirty-two, responding, 10-76. Three minutes out," he said. Aggravated domestic calls often prove to be the most dangerous for law enforcement officers and require mandatory backup, per department policy.

"Three sixty-one, responding base, five minutes," Rooster chimed in. His siren roared to life.

"Three twenty-one, in route, also five out," Reddy said, his siren blaring.

Two familiar units from the Gwinnett County Sheriff's Office were nearby.

"GCSO Chapel providing back up, PD, over?" Officer Chapel's younger brother, Greg's voice, came over the radio.

"Roger that SO. PD appreciates the assist," dispatch relayed.

"GCSO Chapel, H. L., and one, also responding, PD. Over?" Chapel's father also responded. All three Chapel men were assigned to that section of the county, representing two law enforcement agencies. That night, they led the mini task force of six law enforcement officers (LEOs) responding to the aggravated domestic going down on Power Avenue.

Officer Chapel and Sergeant Stone, along with Chapel's father and the rookie riding with him, heard screams coming from an apartment. They converged outside the apartment and made entry with the assist of Michael Chapel's size thirteen triple E tactical boot, which made splinters out of the locked and bolted solid core door. Entry achieved.

Inside, they found two local thugs suspected by both law enforcement agencies of being involved in drugs and other criminal activity. Both bullies were roughing up Amy Parker, Emogene Thompson's neighbor. Parker was a regular at the American Inn, the local mecca of ill-repute, believed by GCPD to be a hub for prostitution and drug trades, and thus. known to the officers.

"Put your hands where we can see 'em, gentlemen!" Sergeant Stone advised as the four officers entered the premises, weapons drawn and ready.

Amy Parker was crying, her face bruised. Mascara mixed with blood ran from the broken skin around her right eye. Once the officers entered the apartment, her two attackers immediately backed away with their hands in the air. Parker, no longer under siege, turned on the police.

"What the hell, officers? Why are y'all breakin' in here?" Parker screeched. "We ain't done nothin' wrong!"

"Ma'am, it appears that these men were assaulting you," Officer Michael Chapel said.

"Ain't nobody assaultin' nobody here, and nobody asked you pigs to come kickin' doors down!" Parker screamed. She pointed at Chapel. "And we don't need this big Terminator lookin' bastard in here, harassin' us like he was harassin' my neighbors earlier today!"

"This one's a piece of work," Stone informed the other members of the task force, "but if she refuses to press, there's nothing much for us to do here." No arrests were made, and no charges filed. After pronouncing her a 'piece of work,' Sergeant Stone led the officers from the apartment, unaware that the beating Parker was receiving and all of her actions from that day forward would have a profound impact on Officer Michael Chapel and the entire Northside Precinct.

 **Three**

S*unday, April 4, 1993, started as routine as any day* that Officer Chapel
was on duty. However, the seemingly innocuous events of the day
would begin to set the stage for an ominous future. After breakfast at
home, he spent a little time playing with his kids, Chad and Chelsea.
Finally, he kissed his wife, Eren, goodbye, threw his gym bag into the
trunk of his squad car, and headed for Iron World. Duty started at 1400.

After roll call and briefing, Chapel checked his precinct mailbox. Rooster
handed him a note from the Day Sergeant, R. H. Winderweedle, Hollywood as he was known at the precinct, asking Chapel to follow up with
Emogene Thompson at his first opportunity.

Chapel and his patrol partners were scheduled to patrol the area around
Lake Lanier. It was the first warm spring weekend in '*Hotlanta.*' Naturally, Lake Lanier would be hopping, but first things first.

"I've got to make this stop on the way out to Lanier, per Hollywood,"
Chapel informed Stone as they exited the precinct together. "I'll catch up
with you guys at Ellen's."

"Roger that, Chapel," crowed the Rooster, who had skipped breakfast
again, and asked the crew to do an earlier than normal chow stop.

On his way to the Craig Drive home, where he had answered the burglary call the day before, a motorist in a red Jeep blew through the stop

sign at Pass Court and nearly hit Chapel's squad car. His lights instantly went on, and Chapel notified dispatch of a 10-37 on Craig Drive. Chapel let the petrified driver off with a warning and proceeded the short distance to the Thompson's residence. He pulled up to the curb at the driveway's skirt and started up the same path to the front door.

"Hi, officer!" came the greeting from a familiar face standing outside of the trailer next door. Parker waved as if they were old friends. Amy was sporting a cut above her right cheek, a black eye, and a bruise purpling half her face. *Nope. Nobody assaultin' nobody*, Chapel thought.

"Howdy, Ms. Parker," Chapel managed. He wondered how this could be the same girl who had called him the terminator, among a few other choice words, less than twenty-four hours earlier. *Whatever,* he thought to himself.

He knocked on the trailer door. It did not open as quickly as the day before. When Ms. Thompson finally peered through the screen. She seemed surprised to see him. "Is everything alright, Officer Chapel?"

"Just following up as requested, ma'am. Have you decided to press charges against your son?"

"I just can't do that, Officer. I can't put my boy back in jail. But I know how you helped my friend Marsha get her daughter into rehab and recover all her stolen jewelry a few months ago. Can't you help me without taking him to jail, like you did for Marsha?"

"Well, ma'am, that was a bit of a different situation," he said. "First, Miss Smith was a minor and hooked up with this same little crew next door, if I recall. And she stole jewelry, not money. Money has a way of disappearing fast."

Ms. Thompson shook her head. "That Amy, she is a good girl, but some of her friends seem a little rough. Mikey's over there right now." In her eyes, Chapel saw a mother's love that made it hard for him to simply walk away. He had to do something.

"I guess I could try to scare Mikey, run a little operation we call *the Boo.*"

Three

"The Boo? What's that?" Ms. Thompson asked.

"I could show up at Michael's place of employment. I believe he works at Subway?"

Ms. Thompson nodded. "At the Buford Mall."

"I'll tell him that some of the bills and paper bank bands from the money have been recovered. The fingerprint analysis on the bands is underway, and it will be back from the crime lab soon. Considering the anticipated results, he will be arrested for the felony unless, of course, he wants to come forward, apologize to his mother, and help her recover the missing funds."

Ms. Thompson thought this was a brilliant plan, and she asked Officer Chapel to proceed.

For the second consecutive day, Officer Chapel left Craig Drive, summoned both times from a female caller, identifying herself as Emogene Thompson. This would be the last time Chapel had any contact with Emogene Thompson.

While Chapel talked with Ms. Thompson, one of Amy Parker's cohorts, Barry Graham, took a Polaroid picture of Chapel's squad car parked in front of the trailer.

Following Emogene Thompson's murder, frequently interviewed Amy Parker and District Attorney Danny Porter contended to the press that Chapel had been stalking the victim as part of his 'master plan.' Barry Graham told police he 'forgot' why he took the photo of Chapel's car and was unsure why he sent it to police.

Unfortunately, Barry Graham never got to tell his story or answer questions in a court of law. Shortly after being identified as a possible defense witness, he allegedly committed suicide in January 1995, six months before the trial.

According to GCPD Sergeant Steve Cline and the *Atlanta Journal-Constitution*, SWAT responded to a hostage situation at Barry Graham's home. When Graham's wife, the alleged hostage, walked out the front door unharmed, twenty-five members of the GCPD SWAT stormed the house after deploying a flash-bang grenade. Cline told the *AJC* that Graham must have already been dead. Nobody heard the shotgun blast.

Twenty minutes after agreeing to meet Rooster for an early lunch and six minutes after Chapel left Craig Drive, he notified dispatch, "10-7, Ellen's on Main." He ran the errand per Winderweedle, made a traffic stop, and joined his watch partners for chow. He ate his meal with his watch partners, utterly unaware of what had just been set in motion.

On Wednesday, April 7, Officer Chapel began his evening patrol with a drive-by to the Subway Sandwich Shop in the Bufford Mall Shopping Plaza across from the American Inn.

"Good evening," the six-foot-seven behemoth said as he entered. He nodded to the two familiar workers behind the counter.

"You want to step outside and talk to me, Mr. Thompson?" He asked sternly.

"Umm, sure, I guess," the scrawny young man stuttered as he took off his apron. He asked his co-worker, Amy Parker, to cover for him. She obliged, but not before mumbling something about the terminator and police harassment.

"What's up, um Officer, um Chapel?" A bead of sweat formed across his upper lip.

"That's right, Mikey. Officer Chapel. Let's cease with the nonsense, and you tell me what you did with all that money you stole from your mother."

"I stole? Wait, um, my mom already told ya someone broke in, man; and I told ya, I don't know nothin' 'bout that!" Thompson said. He repeatedly swiped at his brow line.

"Cut the crap, buddy," Chapel said. "You and I both know that nobody broke into that trailer, and burglars don't steal only half of the money they find. Now, do they, Mikey?"

Three

"I don't know 'bout all that, man. I just know I didn't do it!" He shoved his fisted hands in his pockets.

"Well, Mikey, I've recovered a bank band from the money you stole and a couple of the bills you gave to your drug dealer." He flipped open his case notebook to reveal three $100 bills and a couple of travelers' checks, his stash, set aside to buy a turkey rifle. "And I'm about to arrest the lot of you if you don't come clean and help me recover the rest of your momma's money."

Thompson was nervous and jittery as he was the first time Chapel encountered him. During the trial, the prosecution would claim he was upset over a show-cause order for non-payment of child support. He claimed this, not Officer Chapel's interrogation, was why he was so anxious and stressed out. However, Thompson mentioned nothing at the time he and Chapel spoke. Instead, he maintained his innocence, and since his mother was unwilling to press charges, there was little Chapel could do. Chapel warned Thompson to come clean before it was too late and threatened to return with a warrant for his arrest.

"You can't arrest me for somethin' I didn't do," Thompson said and abruptly turned. "I gotta go back to work." He stumbled over his feet and almost fell through the glass door.

"Careful, son. Nerves will do that to you." Chapel said.

Officer Chapel left a shaken Michael Thompson at the Subway Sandwich Shop. He would not see him again until two and a half years later when Thompson would take the stand as the star witness for the prosecution and turn a pointed finger at Chapel.

 **Four**

*T*he *GCPD patrolman waved Lisa Taylor's vehicle to a stop.* He tipped the brim of his trooper hat as he approached. "Evening, ma'am."

"Did I do something wrong, officer?" Taylor inquired. Taylor's was the first vehicle pulled over at the Gwinnco Muffler Shop checkpoint.

"No, ma'am," the patrolman said. "We're investigating an incident that happened over here last night." He pointed to the entrance of the muffler shop. Two Gwinnett County Patrol cars were parked near the spot where a Lincoln Continental was found twelve hours earlier with Emogene Thompson's dead body resting in the front seat.

Upon questioning, Taylor said she had seen a dark-colored, possibly gray, older model sedan on the shoulder of the road near the muffler shop the night before. She traveled down Peachtree Industrial Boulevard at approximately 9:15 pm headed to her home in Buford.

"Chapel!" Rooster shouted from across the highway. Officer Chapel unfolded his six-foot-seven frame and stepped from the blue striped patrol car, strikingly like several other GCPD patrol cars on the scene, to assist with the roadblock. "I need you and Reddy to work the southbound traffic," Rooster ordered.

"Roger that, boss," Chapel said. "Reddy's a no show, though. Haven't seen him and couldn't reach him on the com."

"Damn it!" Stone spat the words. "I gave him a direct order. So, where the hell is he?"

"Don't know, boss," Chapel said. "He's not on a call that I'm aware of. I'll keep reaching out."

"Keep me posted." Rooster said, clearly frustrated that one of his reports had ignored a direct order.

"Roger that." Officer Chapel moved into position at the southbound traffic stop.

Over the next week, including the following Thursday, from 2100 to 2200, give or take thirty minutes, the GCPD conducted roadblocks on Peachtree Industrial Boulevard as they looked for possible witnesses to the events of April 15, 1993.

Numerous witnesses came forward and claimed they saw a police car sitting in the Gwinnco parking lot as early as 8:45 pm. Witnesses could not agree on the description or details of the patrol car and its occupant. Some saw blue lights, and some did not. Most saw a boxy-looking mid-eighties style car with a large yellow stripe. Two witnesses described the eight to ten cars at the roadblock. Some said that headlights were on; others said they were off. Others said the dome light was on. One witness, traveling southbound, described a large man with brown hair and wearing a white shirt inside the vehicle. Remarkably, the witness was able to grab those details while traveling southbound, at night, 'at or near the speed limit,' from over 100 feet away, and under rainy conditions.

Another witness, Ronald Flashner, traveling southbound at a little before 10:00 pm, reported seeing the victim's car in the driveway with another big vehicle backed up behind it. He reported seeing three to four people moving around the cars. He stated that a lot of smoke emanated from the vehicle facing the road and created a cloud across the highway, making it difficult to describe any of the people at the scene.

The local media focused on the possible law enforcement connection and claimed GCPD had reason to believe a police officer was involved. As

soon as the explosive news hit the airwaves, it made its way up the organization chart within the police department. The press and the department were hotter than hell and the lower half of Georgia.

"This isn't Bogotá, damn it, Latty!" Deputy Chief of Police Carl White
screamed at his acting Chief of Detectives. "We can't have our officers
out running around executing citizens, by god!" White, an imposing
figure within the GCPD hierarchy, smoldered behind his cluttered desk.

"We're working it, sir. We're following some leads and may be able to
start making some arrests soon," John Latty said, leaning against the
closed office door, determined not to fail this time.

"Arrests?" White barked back. "Are you telling me we have multiple cops
involved in killing this poor woman?"

"Well, no sir, we don't know that," Latty explained. "But the officer we
suspect is involved, Morgan, is allegedly tied up with a drug and prostitution operation, money laundering, and possibly into creepy pornog-
raphy. We have reason to believe a few other cops might be involved in
some of those activities, sir."

"Mary, mother of God!" White said. "Who the hell is running that
Northside Precinct, Pablo, damn, Escobar? I need an arrest, Latty! I need
to perp-walk a police officer, not some drug ring, not some flunkies, and
not a bunch of perverted LEOs. Give me the cop who was at the scene.
He is the shooter. He is the bad guy! Let's put his ass behind bars!"

"Count on it, sir," Latty said. "We'll get our man."

"Make it stick this time, Latty. We don't need another damn Day brother's fiasco!" White yelled, referring to one of Latty's own and the department's most significant black eyes in recent years.

Lieutenant Latty was accused of witness coercion and bribery of multiple
convicted felons. Accusations included allegedly providing cocaine and
marijuana to state prisoners, Billy Joe Swafford, and Ronnie Simonds in
exchange for testimony against the Day brothers.

Herman Day and his younger brother, Bobby Lee Day, were charged in the cold case with the 1974 robbery and murder of a Buford package store clerk, Elfred Poucher. Charges against Bobby Lee Day were dropped shortly after Herman Day was acquitted by a jury of his peers.

According to the *Atlanta Journal-Constitution*, Lieutenant Latty was also the central figure in an unprecedented number of unsolved murders in Gwinnett County. A headline in 1986 about the Gwinnett Police Department being puzzled by thirty unsolved murders was not helpful to Latty's upward mobility within the department. Nevertheless, he would eventually be the Head Detective before being demoted again. Simultaneously, the number of unsolved cases continued to grow, and the unsolved article ink continued to flow at the *AJC*. Despite Latty's obsessive and sometimes imaginative drive to solve the cases, answers were few and far between.

Latty, and his understudy, Jack Burnette, resorted to every means necessary to 'clear the board' and solve cases.

In the Elfred Poucher case, they tried to turn Billy Joe Swafford into a snitch with disastrous results. While Swafford's brother Ronnie was in jail, facing burglary charges, and Billy Joe was on probation, Latty offered to talk to the District Attorney on their behalf if Billy Joe would help the GCPD convict the Day brothers. When that plan did not work, Latty and Burnette told Officer Michael Chapel that he would get a call in his zone from Swafford's residence on Power Avenue.

"Make a big ole deal out of it, scare the bejesus out of him, and tell 'em you're a callin' in the big guns," said Jack Burnette, one of Chapel's mentors. He spat a wad of Redman chewing tobacco.

Latty added, "Tell 'em Dixie Mafia is after him. That'll get Billy Joe worked up."

The next day, as promised, dispatch radioed Chapel with an eighty-six – domestic – on Power Avenue. When Chapel arrived, he found a crudely fashioned and slightly burned wooden cross in Billy Joe Swafford's front yard. Swafford's wife and Billy Joe himself were already scared when Chapel folded himself out of his patrol car and notified dispatch, 10-7 (*arrival on scene*).

Four

"Any idea who could have done this, Mr. Swafford?" Chapel asked, thinking to himself, *you wouldn't believe it if I told you.*

"I know damn well who done it!" Billy Joe offered, "It was one of them bastard Day boys!"

Chapel refrained from laughing, but was also a little put off that Burnette and Latty put him in the middle of this unsavory ploy. "Day boys running with the Dixie Mafia these days? Come on, Billy Joe, that cross is a recognizable signature."

"Dixie Mafia! Aw, man, the Day boys are running with them?" Swafford's fear escalated.

"Dixie Mafia will come 'fer my whole family since we got beef with them Day boys. Shit, Officer, you gotta help me!"

"I wouldn't worry about your family, Mr. Swafford," Chapel said, concerned the ruse had worked a little too well. "The Dixie Mafia isn't coming for your family. I would just worry about your beef with the Day brothers. So, let's think about how we can help you with that situation."

"Shit, I reckon their whole family got a beef with my whole family, seems like, even though we might be kinfolk, cousins or something," Swafford said. Indeed, Latty would later describe the two factions as occasional partners in crime while at other times feuding over girlfriends and the proceeds of their criminal enterprises.

"I wasn't aware of that, Mr. Swafford. So maybe it's best if I turn this over to our detective division," Chapel said, ready to complete his assignment and get away from the train wreck he saw coming down the tracks. "I'm gonna call Lt. Latty. He'll be the best one to handle a dangerous situation like this."

After the successful ruse, Lt. Latty got his snitch, and an early running of the *Gwinnett County Railroad* would wind its way down the tracks to utter failure and total derailment.

Billy Joe Swafford found himself back in jail and reached out to Latty. Latty turned Billy Joe Swafford and several of his fellow felonious convicts into states' witnesses. When they got on the witness stand and placed their right hand on the Bible, instead of delivering the goods against the Day brothers, they spilled the beans on Latty's coercion tactics.

Swafford and his cohorts reported that Latty signed Swafford out of jail, chauffeured him home, allowed him to have a conjugal visit with his wife, then bought him a steak dinner while he fed Swafford the facts of the case so that he could sound like a credible witness. Latty then helped Swafford smuggle drugs into the county lockup.

The case blew up in the District Attorney's face. Fledgling Assistant District Attorney Danny Porter, suggested that the DA's office run its own parallel investigations in all major or high-profile cases where Latty and Burnette were involved in the future.

Undaunted, Burnette and Lt. Latty continued their attempts to solve their case no matter what it took. Lt. Latty would tell the *Atlanta Journal-Constitution*, "As far as I'm concerned, it doesn't matter where you get your information from, as long as enough people tell you the same thing."

Those words would prove prophetic in Chapel's case as Latty and Burnette resorted to any means and any source available once their circumstantial case against Chapel began to fall apart. Assistant Chief White's apparent instructions and decision to place Latty and Burnette in charge of the investigation of the murder of Emogene Thompson sealed Michael Chapel's fate regardless of where the facts led.

Five

*A*cting *Chief Detective Latty believed* the Emogene Thompson case to be the only one that mattered. Chief White amped up the pressure, and Latty felt the heat. He assembled a group of high-ranking detectives for a roadside meeting off Highway 20. "What do we have on Morgan?"

"Not much, sir," Lead Investigator Burnette said, "He fits the description of the cop at the scene but so does about 90% of the department. Other than that, we ain't got nothing tying Morgan to the scene or the victim at this point. We all know he's dirtier than bedsheets in a brothel, but we got nothing on 'im."

"Well, nothing doesn't work! We need to clear this case off the board! Now, get me something I can give to the Chiefs to get them off my back," Latty pushed.

"Well, we can tie another officer to the victim and the money," Detective Steve Cline said.

"Go on," Latty said.

"Chapel was on duty. It's his beat." Cline said, shining the light on Chapel.

Steve Cline made his case with trademark cockiness. "As you know, he investigated the alleged burglary at the Thompson residence three weeks ago, which he failed to report."

"Chapel?" Burnette said. "That's gonna be a hard sell. He's like our *Kindergarten Cop* up there on the Northside."

"Well, yeah, but we can prove he was having financial problems, IRS, small business debt. So, he needed the money."

"How could we know that already?" Burnette asked. "We've just started this investigation."

"Browning from IA shared those details; they already have Chapel under investigation in that roid-rage thing," Cline answered. And then Cline threaded his theory with a lie.

"We also have reason to believe he was supposed to meet the vic with her money—on or about the date in question—under the guise of finding her missing funds from the initial call."

Burnette did not bite. "I'm aware of Amy Parker's statements to that effect Steve, but it's real hard to call her a credible witness. We got no proof that Chapel did any of that." To punctuate, he spat chew.

"He was stalking her." Steve Cline said, building his theory. "He was determined to get his hands on that money!"

"Hold up," said Burnette. "You're a-tellin' me Michael Chapel was so hard up for a little cash that he done lured some old lady to a parkin' lot on the side of a busy highway, with tons of witnesses passing by, on his beat, and in uniform, with his numbered patrol car lit up like a dad-burn Christmas tree, and shot her? Come on now! Mike ain't stupid!" Burnette spat again.

Cline said, "Well, Jack, somebody in a GCPD car, lit up like a Christmas tree, in uniform shot this lady in the head on the side of a busy highway, with tons of witnesses passing by!" Cline said, "And your buddy Chapel is the only one who was, by my account, secretly investigating her, and with knowledge of the money. We know from a witness that he arranged to meet her at the muffler shop!"

Five

"And!" Cline wound up for the big close. "We know the dude is jacked-up on steroids. That's why IA is all over him! Just look at 'im. He's a jacked-up roid-monster, just like Jim Bob Batsel!"

Latty wryly smiled and settled back. "Sounds like we've got our man, gentlemen. As hard as it is to believe a guy like Chapel could be that stupid or commit such a horrible crime, it all fits."

"You gotta be shittin' me," Burnette said.

After thirty minutes of back-and-forth, Latty began to conclude the conclave. "Okay. So, the focus is 100% on Chapel, gentlemen. Keep the investigation close to the vest. Limit PD involvement to this group as much as possible. We don't want a bunch of uniforms going to bat for one of their own."

"What about Shelton, sir? Dave Baker and Barnhart have got a lot on him, and then there's the vic's son. They think they're both involved somehow."

"It's Chapel, Burnette! Focus on Chapel! The Chiefs are riding my ass like I'm Seattle Slew! Now, let's get the job done!"

They would get the job done. One after another, witnesses reported seeing a police car on the final night of the roadblocks. And even though statements were vague and contradictory, it was enough for Latty's team.

It was 9:25 pm on Thursday, April 22. Three witnesses said they were on their way home from evening service at the local Kingdom Hall, their place of worship, as they had been the previous week on the night of the murder.

Sean Charles said, "I saw a boxy white police car facing Peachtree Industrial and a man sitting in the police car."

"Did you get a good look at the officer? Can you describe him?"

"Well, I don't think I saw him well enough to describe his features," Charles said, "but he was wearing a white shirt and looking down."

35

Maryann Johnsa, who was riding in the car, described the scene in nearly the same manner as Stacey Turner, the driver. All three were from the same congregation at Kingdom Hall.

At the same time, investigators followed up with a local businessman, Karl Kautter, identified by his friend and the driver of the car he traveled in on the night of the murder, Paul Omodt.

"I saw a white male in a yellow rain slicker walking up to the brown Lincoln with a flashlight in his right hand, looked like someone getting a ticket," Kautter said.

"Yes, sir," Kautter continued, "the flashlight was on."

"Can you describe the man with the flashlight?" The officer asked.

"Well, he appeared to be an officer of some sort. I couldn't really see his face, but he was about six-foot, medium build," Kautter reported.

"Would you say he was a huge man?"

"Well, you could probably say large, maybe six-one, a little bit stocky."

Paul Omodt would say 'maybe six-two' in a statement. At trial, he clarified—six foot and drew the comparison to his height at five-eleven.

Investigators could now place a 'large' GCPD officer at the scene, who they would describe as 'very large' despite the witness statements, and it was time to make their move.

On Friday, April 23, Chief Bolden and Assistant Chief White were intensely focused. They let the hierarchy within GCPD know that Michael Chapel's arrest was imminent. Anyone defending Chapel would be shut down. GCPD rank and file were ordered to present a united front.

Chief Bolden, Assistant Chief White, and Assistant Chief Doss hosted a team meeting at GCPD Headquarters that afternoon. In attendance were Captain. R. L. Davis, Sgt. Steve Cline, Lt. John Latty, District Attorney Investigators Dave Baker and Glenn Teantino, and Lead Investigator Jack Burnette. Burnette, now on board, kept meeting minutes in his case notebook.

Chief Bolden opened the meeting. "Gentlemen, later today, we intend to bring Officer Michael Chapel in for interrogation, after which he will be arrested for the robbery and murder of Emogene Thompson. This action is no small matter for this department, and our darkest days may be ahead. I know many of you are close to Chapel. We're all brothers in blue, but the public demands justice, and we're going to give it to them!"

Assistant Chief White took over. "First order of business—Investigator Baker tells me the DA still needs a scene witness. Can no one place Chapel at the scene?"

"Karl Kautter is as close as we have," Capt. Davis said to the team. "He was riding with another witness, Paul Omodt. They saw a 'very large' cop with a flashlight looking into the victim's car. Shortly after they passed, a cop car, they assume the same one, caught up to them, rode alongside for a bit, and then turned just past Highway 20."

"Did Kautter get a good look at this 'very large' cop?" Dave Baker asked.

"Well, he's a little cloudy on that. I'm pretty sure he was impaired—alcohol and drugs, most likely."

"That's not going to help," Baker said. "I'm not really hearing anything that ties Chapel to this crime. Gentlemen, I understand your theory that he stalked her, then lured her to the muffler shop. If you can prove that, then he's your man. However, you haven't produced any direct evidence of Chapel soliciting a meeting, and you don't have a single credible witness that can place Chapel at or near the scene."

Latty nearly exploded. "You'll have your damn witnesses! I've got a whole carload of church-going Christians that described him to a tee. This is happening, Gentlemen. We have a solid case, and we're going to bring Chapel in."

White took over. "Latty and Burnette will get Chapel to talk, or at least give us incriminating evidence. Let's just talk about the interrogation and settle down."

Michael Chapel

From Lead Detective Jack Burnette's handwritten case notebook meeting minutes:

(a) *May want to manufacture wit.* (Witnesses)
(b) *Offer him a way out – maybe the victim carrying a gun*
(c) *Interview Room*
(d) *Interview needs to be very private – don't parade into headquarters.*
(e) *Feed facts, talk about burglary, theft of money*
(f) *Talk about what a good officer he is and how the vict* (Victim)

The Chief of Police and the Gwinnett County Police Department's highest-ranking officials prepared Latty and Burnette to interrogate Officer Chapel. These men would set him at ease, be his friend, feed him the facts, manufacture witnesses, confuse him, then give him a way out—not a way out of prison, but maybe a way to avoid electrocution in Georgia's *Old Sparky*. Chapel did not have a chance. As far as GCPD was concerned, the story was written. The end.

At the conclusion of this meeting, Dave Baker's involvement in the Chapel case and the investigation into Dennis Shelton and Michael Thompson ostensibly ended.

On Monday, April 26, 1993, a directive was issued on Chief Bolden's letterhead addressed to the Records and Property Manager. It instructed that only members of the listed team could have access to case evidence, effective immediately. Dave Baker had been replaced on the team by Investigator Greg Browning.

Six

*U*naware of the black cloud hanging over his head, Michael Chapel started another routine day on Friday, April 23, 1993. The climate around the precinct was toxic. Chapel heard J. P. Morgan was a suspect. The Sugar Hill Marshall, Chris Robertson, passed by the precinct a couple of days before and told Rooster and Chapel that he (the Marshall) was a suspect.

Brian Reddy was prodded on multiple occasions to give a supplemental report on his whereabouts after leaving the firehouse the night of the murder. Rooster reported seeing Reddy leave in the direction of the crime scene that was in his zone, just after 10 pm.

Reddy made a log entry shortly after 10 pm that placed him blocks from the murder scene. A log entry Reddy would later call a fabrication, *'just some words on paper.'*

It did not surprise Chapel when the lead investigator, his hunting buddy, whom other officers called Fat Jack, summoned him to headquarters over the com. Reddy, H. L. Zimmerman, and others at the precinct had been called in at some point during the investigation to account for their whereabouts and provide any details associated with or connected to the victim, the murder, or the investigation team's prime suspect, Michael Chapel.

Chapel never considered himself a suspect and did not fathom that the entire power structure, including the Chiefs, high ranking detectives, Captain Davis, Sergeant Cline, and those charged with investigating him within the GCPD had just spent hours working out a strategy on how to get him to incriminate himself. Nor did he consider that he might need to consult with an attorney.

Chapel contemplated making a quick stop to call his wife, Eren, to let her know he was going in for questioning. However, he decided against giving her something more to worry about. He assumed the questioning would be quick.

"I wasn't planning to lie to you. Mike, I thought you were a good cop," Burnette spat a wad of Redman into a Styrofoam cup and began to show his frustration. Chapel's story remained unchanged through hours of questioning.

"I don't think I'd have been prouder had it been Morgan or Brad, but God, I've got an awful lot of questions." Burnette offered, feigning confusion. He rested his hands one atop the other on the table between them.

"Ask me, Jack," Mike effectively dared his friend. The truth was all he had.

"You've got...," Burnette started to speak and stopped himself. He rose and abruptly left the interview. *"I'll be back in a minute."*

"Let me pick up here," Latty filled the void. *"You're a good cop, Mike. You kick butts and take names like I used to do. People up here know you. They respect you. They trust you. You're kind of the heir apparent up here, you know after I left. But I'm going to be straight with you."*

"I wish somebody would, Lieutenant." Chapel responded sincerely, pushing his fingers through his hair.

"I know you are a very smart man, Mike, high IQ, street smarts, and you know how these investigations go." Latty continued following the script, *"I'm going to give you some facts. We found this woman in her car, shot twice in the head, her ignition is on, battery is dead, thirteen gallons of gasoline in the tank, doors locked, and windows up, except the partially down driver's window. She's in her seat belt and slumped over the middle console, and she's got this flat tire."*

"You know what we make of all that, Mike?" Latty teased with a crumb to the investigation's focus.

"That she knew her killer." Mike shrugged at the obvious answer.

"Exactly," Latty confirmed his prime suspect's answer, *"She trusted that person. Now, you know we also have all these witnesses coming forward, and they see this Gwinnett County Police car on the scene. They see this cop in his big yellow raincoat. This has us upset and worried, Mike."*

"Well, it should, Lieutenant."

"It does all of us, okay?"

"It does me, too." Mike agreed.

"Now, the victim's close friends and associates start to contact us with even more ominous information," Latty keeps feeding. *"They tell us how she had discussed with them how you was investigating her case, you, Michael Chapel, big, muscular, handsome man. Now, Reddy is muscular, but he ain't handsome, so we ruled him out. It's obviously you."* Latty leaned in, his expression one of feigned concern.

"Yes," Mike said, not finding the humor in Latty's pontificating, *"I was dealing with her."*

"Yes, you've told us that," Latty acceded, *"but these people say you told her you needed to meet to compare $100 bills, you arranged a meeting."*

"No, I never told her that, whatsoever!" Chapel defended himself against the hearsay.

Latty was feeding GCPD's narrative to Officer Chapel for over an hour when he promised triumphantly, *"I'm fixing to hit you with the last piece of information."*

Mike stared into his hands, tracing the lines in his palms, *"Please do."* He sat up straight and looked directly at Latty.

"You were seen there." Latty let loose his manufactured bomb, *"You were identified."*

"At Gwinnco?" Mike was puzzled. *"I don't see how."* Mike threw his head back, looking towards the heavens. *Something's gotta make more sense than this line of crap,* Mike almost said aloud.

"You've been identified, Mike," Latty lowered the boom. *"These men saw you. You were there, holding your flashlight leaning down over the victim's car when they passed by Gwinnco. They thought someone was getting a ticket and didn't think anything of it as they proceeded on up PIB."*

"Now, you got the call to Arden Drive at 9:56 pm," Latty offered a detail of Mike's alibi.

"Uh-huh?" Chapel held comment until his interrogator fashioned an actual question.

"Well, you got back in your patrol car, sped on up PIB, and caught up to those men that had just seen you. You caught up to them and paused and then shot on through the light and turned just past Highway 20."

"Me?" Mike was distrustful at this point.

"You," Latty confirmed with a nod.

"Well, they're wrong!" Chapel vehemently protested. *"Absolutely mistaken. That is not me."*

"Now you're telling us that you were with Reddy, with Stone from 8:30 pm. Y'all carried on over at the firehouse until you received this call, and you went to check on your gym?"

"Uh-huh." Mike agreed with those details.

"We're in there interviewing them now. Mike, we've got Reddy right down there, now. What's he going to tell us, Mike?"

"They will tell you the same thing. I know what you're saying. It's circumstantial. It doesn't look good, but ..."

Six

"It's not circumstantial, Mike," Latty proclaimed. "Let me tell you. It's not circumstantial when someone picks you out of a photo lineup. That's not circumstantial! You are looking at a murder charge, Mike."

"I… I realize that Lieutenant, what can I say?"

"Tell me the truth," Latty demanded.

"That is the truth, Lieutenant." Chapel insisted. "I did not kill no one. That's… I've told you everything I know about the situation. Granted, it's fucked up. I don't know what else to tell you. That's the truth. I don't know what to tell you now, but …" He dropped the thought.

"Mike, could it be… could it be that you arranged to meet her there to discuss this case, and she responded in some kind of violent way." Latty followed the planned interrogation script and offered a way out, a way to soften the blow. He talked about Mike's size and skill, training, intellect, and maybe for a split second, something just got out of hand.

"Of course not. I don't know what to say. I didn't do it. I wasn't there, it…. I wasn't there." Mike was clearly more uncomfortable with where the interrogation was headed than the small chair he endured for the last several hours. The interrogation had lasted well beyond his original estimation. Glad I didn't call Eren. She'd be going crazy by now.

"You wasn't where you said you was." Latty detonated another bomb. "You wasn't where you said you was, Mike. That alibi is gone as soon as we talk to these people tonight."

"I'm… good." Mike reassured, "I'm glad of it. We're going to get this cleared up tonight because that's where I was, that's what I was doing, that's where I went, that's what I did. It's as simple as that, Lieutenant." Mike slapped his legs in certainty of immediate vindication.

Latty painstakingly walked Mike back through the details of the whole case as GCPD saw it. Throughout, he misrepresented facts that painted an ugly picture for Chapel, insistent that Mike had not written a report or logged the calls to hide his contact with the victim. Both calls originated from the department and therefore could not be hidden. Latty

43

insisted that all these witnesses described him, and one of them picked him out of a lineup.

Chapel's watch partner and self-described good friend, Officer Brian Reddy, gave Sergeant Cline his statement. Reddy claimed that he had not seen Chapel on the night in question after 2030. Reddy affirmed that he, Chapel, and Stone had met at the church as Chapel had described but then stated he and Stone went to the firehouse without Chapel.

"You wasn't there, Mike!" Finally, Burnette was back and insisted, *"Tell the truth, why would Brian lie?"*

"I don't know, Jack," Chapel continued to respond in shock, *"He's mistaken. He's mixing his dates or something. I was there picking on his dumb ass about not knowing what county he lives and works in!"*

"You wasn't there, Mike!" Burnette repeated over and over.

"I was there, Jack, ask the firemen, ask Stone!" Chapel pleaded over and over.

"I will, Mike," Burnette promised, *"you can take that to the bank."*

More forceful and direct, Latty insisted that Mike was not at the firehouse. Latty's facts emphasized that from 2100 to 2156, Chapel was at the Gwinnco Muffler Shop. He laid in wait for Emogene Thompson and murdered her at approximately 2145, sped away nine minutes later to answer the call at Arden Drive. He would be positively identified by a witness Latty described as *'not being manufactured.'*

"Jack Burnette wouldn't manufacture anything," Latty clarified.

"I'm not suggesting he did, Lieutenant," Chapel felt terrible for his friend, Jack, *"I'm just telling you the truth, and it isn't working. I was at the firehouse."* He made direct eye contact with Latty, who shook his head to avoid Chapel's glare.

"You wasn't there, Mike," Latty repeated over and over.

"I was there, Lieutenant!" Chapel responded over and over.

Six

At one point, Latty compared Chapel's situation to that of the infamous Day boys. It was not lost on Michael that the Day boys had been accused of murder and later exonerated because Latty had manufactured the only evidence against them. The case was created from whole cloth and disintegrated in the courtroom.

After hours of this badgering, Latty stepped out of the room while Burnette insisted that Mike was lying. Reddy's statement proved it by disproving his alibi. This witness saw him. Many witnesses saw him and his car. Emogene's girlfriends all heard the victim say this or that about a meeting with him. Latty returned three hours into the accusations of murder, armed robbery, and dishonesty about his whereabouts.

"Well, Mike," Latty interrupted, *"it appears that Reddy was mistaken. You were at the firehouse."*

Finally! Chapel thought to himself and began to feel a sense of relief. Finally, the truth comes out! He ran his hands through his black hair and sighed in relief.

"However," Latty continued, *"You left the firehouse. So, your statement about being at the firehouse is right, but you left."*

Undaunted by the revelation of Officer Reddy's lie and the shrinking window of opportunity, Latty and Burnette plowed forward. They simply adjusted their narrative and continued their mission.

"Mike," Burnette explained, *"we're at the point, as I see it, that the big question to be answered is why. I don't even think we're at a negotiation point on if, not right now."*

They would not negotiate on their position, no matter what the evidence showed or did not show. The decision was made. As far as the GCPD was concerned, Michael Chapel was guilty. This interrogation was merely a formality, an opportunity to feed the facts, set the narrative, and hopefully get the accused to incriminate himself. Through it all, they prepared for the coming press conference, media blitz, and judicial railroad that was on its way down the tracks.

Michael Chapel

Sergeant D. E. Stone would corroborate Chapel's alibi that night, confirming to Captain Davis that all three Northside officers, himself, Chapel, and Reddy, had gone to the Firehouse after the 2030 meeting at the church. Chapel remained until nearly 2200, when he left to deal with a domestic call and run his nightly check on his gym business on Moreno Street. Stone said that he left twenty minutes after Chapel and went next door to the precinct where he phoned his wife. Precinct phone records indicated this call home took place at 2217.

Stone would soon be disciplined by the department, demoted, and reassigned, and then he 'remembered' that his initial statement was wrong. He changed his story to match Reddy's second story. Both men's second statements asserted that Chapel left the firehouse around 2130, allowing him a sliver of time to perpetrate the heinous crime.

Burnette would not keep his promise to Chapel. The promise Chapel could take to the bank—the promise of checking his alibi with the firemen. GCPD never interviewed the six firemen directly. They all wrote and signed statements within days of Chapel's arrest. They gave their statements, virtually all indicating that Chapel was at the firehouse from before 2100 until approximately 2200, to their Captain and then waited to hear from GCPD. They would wait for years.

 **Seven**

Eleven o'clock pm came and went, and Eren Chapel began to worry. Her husband was never late, not like this. By 11:30, she called the precinct and asked if her husband had been delayed on a call. Delays were not uncommon, but Michael typically had dispatch relay a message when an ongoing duty pushed him past shift change.

Mike and Eren had a pact. He would never worry her without cause, so when nobody answered the precinct phone, Eren tensed. She left the children with her mother, Nancy West, and drove toward Buford Highway.

"What is going on?" Eren banged on the front door at Precinct Thirteen. "I can see you in there, Rooster! And I know you hear me. Where is my husband, and what is going on?"

Rooster removed himself from view, and Eren Chapel knew that something horrible had happened to her husband of twelve years. Scared, confused, and angry, Eren called police peadquarters from a nearby Waffle House.

"This is Eren Chapel. Can someone tell me where my husband is and just what the heck is going on?" She demanded an answer.

After placing her on hold for several minutes, a Sergeant picked up the line. In a mechanical voice, he said, "Mrs. Chapel, we are sending a car to

47

your residence to pick you up in about an hour. The Chief would like to speak to you directly and let you know what's happening."

"The Chief...what is...," Eren's concern elevated to terror. "Has Michael been...killed?" Her voice broke with the thought.

"We'll send a car, Mrs. Chapel." the drone repeated.

"No, headquarters is about fifteen minutes from here. I'll be there in ten!" She slammed the receiver. Eren was not prepared to wait another minute.

Eren arrived at GCPD Headquarters on Hi Hope Road to find her husband's squad car backed into a space near the CID entrance to the building. She parked in the space one slot over from Michael's patrol car, directly under a twenty-foot-tall light pole illuminating the area.

Eren did not see any visible damage to the vehicle, so she eliminated 'horrible traffic accident' from the list of nightmares threatening her sanity. She looked inside the vehicle and noted the armrest was all the way down and that Michael's pursuit pack was missing. Again, she tensed.

Michael had asked to have the armrest removed due to his size. He could not drive and maneuver comfortably in his 'shop,' as he called it, with the armrest down. Maybe someone else drove it here, she thought.

Inside headquarters, Eren was ushered into a cold and damp interview room—not unlike the one her husband had endured for several hours that day—and was told the Chief would join her shortly. It was eerily quiet and cold at headquarters, especially for late April. She wrapped her arms across her chest and briskly rubbed her forearms.

Mrs. Chapel was a striking presence with penetrating dark brown eyes, black waist-length hair, and perfect posture. Beyond her physical beauty, she exuded grace, intelligence, and strength to all who knew her. She would not be cornered or ignored. Michael Chapel was her husband, and someone was going to tell her what was going on.

Eren, prepared for the worst, expected to meet with Chief Wayne Bolden, but Assistant Chief Carl White greeted her instead. Also present were

Seven

Major Billy Carty, her husband's close friend and Aikido instructor, and a female officer Eren did not know. After some unwelcome hemming and hawing, Assistant Chief White disclosed the news that even in her worst nightmare, Eren could not have imagined.

"Arrested? A press conference? Murder?" Her head was spinning. "Are you insane? This is Michael Chapel we're talking about!"

"It was hard for me to believe as well," Carty said, trying to sound sympathetic. "But the investigation is conclusive, Eren. The Department has no choice here."

"This cannot be real, Billy," Eren said. "You are telling me that Michael Chapel, the straightest and most law-abiding man I've ever known, just decided to up and murder some little old woman on the side of Peachtree Industrial Boulevard. With his service weapon. While on duty. In his police uniform. In front of God and everybody? Have you all lost your damn minds?"

"He didn't use his service weapon, but everything else you just said is what the investigation has concluded, yes." White lowered his eyes. White did not make eye contact for the rest of the meeting.

"Well, what gun did he use?" She turned to her husband's friend. "Billy?" She was through with the under-chief and ignored the female officer. "Because I am not buying the story you all are selling. His service weapon is the only thing he carries unless she was killed with a .50 caliber tank getter. W-e-l-l?" Mrs. Chapel's patience was waning.

"I can't comment any further on an open investigation," Carty informed her.

"This is absurd, Billy! You know as well as I do that Mike did not do this!" She turned back to White, raised her brow, and demanded, "I want to see my husband right NOW!" She folded her arms across her chest and glared in defiance.

"I'm afraid that won't be possible," White said, eyes on the floor.

"And just why not, sir?" Capable of controlling her temper under trying

49

circumstances, Mrs. Chapel teetered on the edge.

"Well, it's not possible right now, Eren," said White. "Since he's the arresting officer for about 40% of our current inmate population, we had to put him in protective custody."

"I know that's right!" Eren snapped sardonically. "It appears my husband is about the only one around this damned department capable of doing any actual police work!"

"I don't think that kind of insinuation—"

"Look. I just need to see my husband, and you better make that happen because I'm not leaving here until you do." She folded her arms across her chest and glared through the man in front of her.

Carty put a hand on her shoulder. "Eren, I will do everything I can to get you in to see him as soon as we can, but it's just not possible at the moment."

Eren shook out from under Billy's hand. Her hardness surprised her. The thought was enough to undam the tears behind the brave front now crumbling as her beloved husband, Michael Chapel, began an inconceivably long incarceration that deprived him of meaningful contact with his family.

During the interrogation, he had been assured that the investigation would continue. He was promised that all attempts would be made to corroborate his story and alibi. That promise proved false as GCPD, and ultimately the District Attorney took steps to oppose his bail and ensure that he remained on lock-down and in protective custody until well after the trial. These actions ensured that he had no opportunity to investigate the case himself or do anything that might help clear his name.

 **Eight**

" *Chapel? Michael Chapel?*" Danny Porter stepped from behind his gleaming mahogany desk. Behind him, matching bookcases ran from floor to ceiling. Less than four months prior, after winning his first term in office, the door frame was removed to prevent dismantling the desk so six movers could situate the mammoth overstatement in his new chambers.

"That's a quantum leap, Dave," Porter scoffed, peering over the rims of his reading glasses. "You went from delinquent repeat-offender Dennis Shelton to highly decorated officer, Michael Chapel!?! Talk to me."

"I agree, sir. It's hard to believe," Dave Baker answered. "I was on my way to get Shelton's arrest warrant signed when I called John Latty to give PD a heads up. Latty sounded crazy, told me to stop cold, said they had Chapel dead to rights."

"So, they like Chapel as the accomplice?" Porter, still confused, removed his glasses.

"Why not proceed on Shelton and get him to flip? We need everything we can get, especially if we're going to convict a cop with Chapel's service record!"

"PD only likes Chapel. No accomplices. They claim he set the whole thing up to rob the lady."

Michael Chapel

"Chapel? They're sure?"

"Latty says the case is airtight, sir."

"It had damn well better be, Baker," Porter said. "All our careers are on the line if this goes south."

"I can't say I'm sold, sir." Baker cautioned, "There is too much evidence on Shelton, and Chapel is a far cry from the medium-built, six-foot cop described by the witnesses."

"This has train wreck written all over it. Let's get Chief Bolden on the phone. I want to hear this from the top." Porter plopped into the oversized black leather chair.

"Melissa, get me Bolden on the line," Porter called to his assistant outside his door, then returned to his chief investigator. "If we arraign on Chapel, there is no turning back, and I'm not turning in my keys for a hunch!"

Dave took a seat across from Porter. He was still in shock over the idea that they would be going after one of Gwinnett's finest, reeling from the fact that he knew Shelton was involved, if not the murderer.

"Sir," Porter's administrative assistant said, peering around the open door, "Chief Bolden says he's not going to have this conversation over the phone. He wants you to meet him at GCPD Headquarters."

"Tell him I'm on my way." He gave Dave a mischievous look. "This had better be good."

While Michael Chapel was being processed and transported to Hall County to await arraignment, the District Attorney and his lead investigator, Dave Baker, met at GCPD Headquarters on Hi Hope Road. Attending were Chief Wayne Bolden, Assistant Chief Carl White, Chief Detective John Latty, Lead Investigator Jack Burnette, and Detective Steve Cline. These men would enthusiastically present contrived evidence against the department's model officer.

Eight

Porter spoke before everyone was in the conference room. "No offense Chief, but PD had better know what the hell they're doing, or there is going to be some kind of hell to pay!"

"My detectives have been all over this case, Danny," Assistant White said. "We've got our ducks in a row."

"We already had a convincing case that this kid Shelton is guilty. You better have some game-changing evidence."

Latty jumped in. "We looked at Shelton, too, but he may have been in that car on prior occasions, so his prints are inconclusive. Moreover, we know there was a LEO at the scene, and we have a witness description of a very large, brown-haired officer on Chapel's beat. And neither Chapel's logs or dispatch can account for his time between 2030 to 2211."

"Have we pulled the dispatch tapes?" Dave Baker asked.
"The tape will be on my desk in the morning," Latty said.

"I'll need chain of custody on that from the second it leaves dispatch."

"Of course, Danny," Latty said as if offended. "We've been at this awhile."

"This is weak. What else have you got?" Porter asked flatly, ignoring Latty's attitude.

"We learned that Officer Chapel was secretly investigating a robbery at the victim's home approximately three weeks ago."

"Secretly? How? Is that really all you have?" Porter was getting impatient.

"No, that's not all," said Latty, then he embroidered the facts. "We also have witnesses asserting that Chapel set up a meeting that day with the victim and asked her to bring the money so he could compare them to the bills he allegedly recovered."

"Well, that's a bombshell!" Porter conceded. "Can you establish that meeting solicitation?"

"We believe we can, sir," Burnette said and offered a theory devoid of evidence. "According to several of her friends and neighbors, she was planning to meet Chapel that night."

"I don't want to hear about what you believe. I want to hear about what you know. What can you prove? Have y'all interviewed these people?" Porter asked.

Before anyone could answer, Dave Baker fired another round of questions, "How did Chapel solicit this meeting? Did he call, or did Dispatch arrange the rendezvous? Can you prove any of this?"

"Exactly!" Porter nodded agreement with Dave, "There are too many holes in this."

"Well, obviously, he didn't arrange it through Dispatch," White said, annoyed.

"What I think Baker is asking for is some record of the phone call. Has anyone pulled the phone records?" Porter asked.

"Well, no, sir," Detective Cline said, looking sheepish. "I can work on that when I get back to the office."

"Don't worry about it," Porter said. "I'll have one of my people track them down."

Burnette introduced his favorite lead. "We also have a witness who was traveling Northbound on Peachtree Industrial who states the officer caught up to him after he passed the scene. He says the officer drove alongside him for 45 seconds. He described Chapel, then picked him out of a line-up."

Porter nodded. "Okay, gentlemen. You have some compelling evidence. But Michael Chapel was the arresting officer on over a third of my cases in this office. I have always found him to be competent and truthful. He is hell on the witness stand, unwavering and credible. Before you ask me to charge and prosecute this man, you need to tie up every loose end, and you have more than a few."

Eight

Latty tried to jump in, but Porter rolled over him. "I need three things to convict; motive, means, and opportunity. If verifiable and he is unaccounted for from 8:20 until 10:11 pm as you indicate, then I admit, that's opportunity."

"That's what I was going to say," said Latty.

"We know the victim was fatally shot with a Charter Arms or Smith and Wesson .38," continued Porter. "Can you put that gun in his hand?"

"We're sure as hell gonna try," said Burnette.

"And finally, I need motive. There's the money, but why would a decorated LEO resort to murder for a few bucks?"

"That's the thing, sir," Latty said, leaning forward. "He needed the money, and fast. He took out a small business loan that was past due, and the IRS was on his ass about his claimed expenses. He was looking at a $4,000 fine. And, frankly, sir, he fits the profile of the 'roid-raging' killer cops in the Atlanta area right now. We've already sent his blood and urine for testing. I guarantee that guy is jacked up on steroids and amphetamines."

"I'll need more than your guarantee, Lt. Latty, but that's a good start if we can prove it. I need y'all to dig into his finances and prove he was in trouble. Also, see if he had any recent infusions."

"Yes, sir!" Cline said.

"The gun?" Porter asked again.

"Well, we're working on that," Latty said. "We're searching his home and the gym he operates starting at 0900. We'll look through his personal lockers at the precinct. We should also check with the range and his fellow officers to see if he's ever used a .38."

"Anything in the patrol car?" Baker asked.

"Not really," Cline said. "We're still processing his personal effects, but nothing stands out."

"Where is the car? Is it in COC?" (*Chain of Custody*)

"Well, yes, sir. It's here at headquarters." Latty did not volunteer that he was unsure if the car, still parked in front of the building, was secured. It would slip his mind again and remain unsecure outside the impound and outside of chain of custody for the next week.

"We've got enough for arraignment and maybe the press," Porter said, "but I need a lot more to convict, gentlemen. Let me be very clear about this. If you are asking me to prosecute Officer Michael Harold Chapel for murder, then every man in this room, including you, Chief Bolden, is laying his career on the line."

"What you have is not enough. I'll do your press conference and arraign Chapel, but you have a lot of work to do. I need an unimpeachable motive, method, and opportunity." He paused to eye every man in the room. "Any questions?"

"No, sir," Latty assured. "You'll have all three!"

Eren and Michael owned a modest house on West Park Place Drive in Lawrenceville, their first home together. The yard filled with color from seasonal flowers in the spring and summer shaded by a stately oak at the front of the house. A blue kiddie pool leaned against the hurricane fence in the backyard. Sheba, the family dog—part Shepard, part Husky— barked at the GCPD officers navigating a boy's bicycle, and pink Big Wheel abandoned at the front door.

Nancy West, Eren's mother, stood in the living room with her arms folded, making eye contact with each officer entering the dwelling. "You officers can search anything you want," she said in her raspy southern drawl. "Just, please don't destroy the place. I am not in the mood to spend my Saturday cleaning up behind you!"

"We'll be as respectful as we can, ma'am," the officer in charge said.

After two and a half hours of combing through Michael Chapel's home under the watchful glare of Nancy West, the lead officer came up with two items to discuss with Jack Burnette, who was in charge of the street-level investigation.

"Ms. West, may I use the phone," an officer asked, pointing to the wall unit near the back door.

Nancy hissed, "You have just fondled my personal intimates and dug through my purse. You rifled the children's toy box and combed through my daughter's cabinets as if expecting to find body parts, but now you need my permission to use the phone? Don't be absurd!" She rolled her eyes. "Use the damn phone."

Jack Burnette picked up after one ring. "What'd you find?"

"A white envelope, sir. It has 'Tips' written on the front." The officer thumbed the roughly five hundred dollars in his hand. "Found it in Mrs. Chapel's nightstand."

"Describe it."

"There are two one-hundred-dollar bills, a few twenties, about seven tens, and the rest are fives and ones," he answered.

"She a waitress?"

"I believe she's a bartender and cocktail waitress at the local Hooters, sir. Would you like me to record the serial numbers on the bills?"

After a few seconds, the officer laid the envelope and its contents on the kitchen counter top. He did not record any serial numbers.

"Also, Mrs. Chapel's mother resides in the home, sir. She owns a shrouded .38 revolver, Smith and Wesson."

"Where'd you find it?"

"We found it on a cabinet shelf in the kitchen. I have possession of the weapon."

"Putting you on hold."

There was a long, uncomfortable pause as the officer absorbed Nancy's piercing glare.

Burnette came back on the line, and soon the officer returned the receiver to the cradle. Without a word, he unloaded the pistol, laid the weapon and ammunition on the same counter as the white envelope, ordered the police officer with the camera to snap a photo of the gun, and said, "Sorry to have disturbed you, ma'am. We're done here."

"I'm no police officer," Nancy said as the officers exited the home, "but what does it say if you are looking for a .38 revolver and a bunch of cash and leave both lying on the kitchen counter in the suspect's house?"

"It says maybe somebody knows the gun and money that they're looking for isn't going to be found at Michael Chapel's place. Have a good day, ma'am." The officer said as he tipped his trooper hat and followed his team out the front door.

Nine

With loose, shoulder-length salt and pepper hair and a looped earring in his left ear, Attorney Walt Britt claimed the chair at the table in the interview room and leaned toward his newly acquired and infamous client. "Mr. Chapel, is it possible that Officer J. P. Morgan set you up?"

Michael eyed the mirrored window behind Britt. Walt told him that the Hall County Jail Commander, Jim Ashe assured him that the microphone was off, and no one was watching or listening to the interview so they could have a constitutionally protected attorney-client privileged conversation.

Chapel's first thought, I can only hope Dad didn't sell the farm to pay this hippy-looking guy. However, Britt's reputation and skill were hard-earned. He knew what he was doing and Chapel was grateful to be in competent albeit unconventional hands.

"Interesting question, Mr. Britt. Why do you ask?"

"Well, a little birdie told me that's what's happening here," Britt said.

"Maybe," Chapel began. "Morgan and I haven't seen eye to eye for some time. I've been looking into some of his nighttime dealings around our shared beat. He's the first shift patrolman; I'm the second. We often run into the same citizens, suspects, and situations, although he seems to have more friendly relationships with the suspects."

"What do you mean?" Britt questioned his client.

Chapel shrugged. "I think he and possibly several other GCPD officers are taking protection payments from the local drug-running ring, Took-ie's crew for starters. And I think they're mixed up in the prostitution and porno rings he's running out of the old American Inn motel. One of those pay by the hour joints. You know what I'm talking about."

Britt nodded. "Go on."

Chapel shifted in the small plastic chair, similar to the one that recently cramped his back and legs for four hours. "Frankly," he said, "on at least two occasions, Morgan knew about planned drug raids that did not involve him. And by the time we arrived, drugs and contraband were cleared out. The perps greeted me like I was Santa Claus with elves. Offered us milk and cookies to go with our search warrants!"

"That lines up with the song my little birdie is singing," Britt said. "My firm will be focusing its investigative efforts on Officer Morgan. We'll get to the bottom of this." Britt pushed a well-used yellow legal pad and pen at Chapel. "I need you to write down all the intel you remember on Morgan and any other cops that might be involved with Morgan or other illegal activities."

"I can't do that."

"Why not?"

"Because this only has three pages left."

Britt smiled and fished out a fresh pad. Chapel filled seven-and-a-half pages.

The following day, Morgan walked into GCPD Headquarters to pick up his paycheck. He also retrieved a note instructing him to contact Jim Ashe. Morgan and Ashe had worked together at GCPD, were good friends, and Jim Ashe would soon be at Morgan's funeral, asked to be a pall bearer.

Nine

Morgan arrived home and made a phone call to the Hall County Jail Commander's office. Ashe would deny taking this seven-minute call in his office, despite the phone records obtained by private investigator Dennis Miller, proving that it had occurred. After the call, Morgan paced his living room and mumbled to himself while his wife plated Chick-fil-a for the family.

"Dinner!" Renee Morgan called. The family gathered around the table; dinner together was a house rule, even if it was take-out.

Renee had never seen her husband in this foul a mood. She tried to tease him out with news about the children's school day. Their preteen daughter had not made the cheer leading squad and was understandably disappointed.

Morgan took a few bites of his sandwich and got up without saying anything. He ignored his family's questions as he pounded the stairs to his home office.

His office was furnished with a desktop computer array that included two screens and video editing and disk replication capabilities, all state-of-the-art for 1993. Officials would later contend the equipment was used for nefarious purposes. He started typing.

After seven or eight minutes, Mrs. Morgan called to her husband from the bottom of the stairs. "Honey, are you okay?" She could hear the tapping keys but got no answer. She waited, then finally returned to the dinner table.

"Daddy's fine," she said to her children. "He's just dealing with a lot of..."

BLAM! A .40 caliber shot rang out from the second floor, followed by a sickening thud.

Morgan's wife instantly knew what had just occurred. Shaken to her core, she hurried her terrified children next door and used that neighbor's phone to call 911.

"I think our subject just killed himself," the private investigator said to Walt Britt over his cellular bag phone. "I'm down the street in my stake-out spot. I heard a gunshot, and fifteen seconds later, his wife and children barreled out of the front door all hysterical like."

"Now, the place is crawling with cops," the Private Investigator continued, "whole damn department. Chiefs are there, White and Bolden, Capt. Davis, Lt. Bishop, Tkacik, a bunch of uniforms, their CSI team; funny thing though, they are all out in the yard. They haven't even let the paramedics in, and the medical examiner just joined the yard party."

"Yes, sir, Tkacik was the first and only one inside for a while. Then they let that Hurst fellow through and the Chiefs, of course," the PI continued to answer questions.

"Yea, Bodie Hurst. I think that's right. I think he's some kind of computer guru or something?"

After being summoned to the scene of Officer J. P. Morgan's apparent suicide, Officer Bodie Hurst, GCPD's "IT Specialist," inspected the blood-spattered computer in Morgan's office, the dead man inches away, and with the leadership of GCPD present and in command of the scene.

Sitting in the same chair that Morgan had fallen from when he took his own life, Bodie Hurst examined, then erased whatever Morgan had typed in the minutes before his last intentional act on Earth. Then he permanently wiped and destroyed the hard drives, and all incriminating evidence vanished.

An internal affairs investigation into other nefarious dealings of Officer Hurst uncovered the incident and led to multiple criminal charges against him, including computer forgery, theft, and trespass. He was charged with four separate counts of violation of oath of office, false swearing, false statements, and multiple counts of robbery. The extent of the evidence, or the contents of a potential confession and suicide note, as well as the contents of the videotapes they removed, is still known only to Hurst, and GCPD leadership.

The medical examiner also described one .38 caliber revolver on Morgan's nightstand, a second gun that matched the caliber identified as the murder weapon in the Emogene Thompson case. Like the one found in the Chapel home, this weapon was never tested or cleared by the state's crime lab, as per investigation protocol. The whereabouts of said weapon, like so much evidence associated with this case, are currently unknown.

"Damn it, Latty," Assistant Chief White screamed at the acting Chief of Detectives.

"We've arrested Chapel, had a big ole loud-ass press conference, and told the whole blasted world that Chapel is the bad guy. And now, Morgan, your previous GCPD suspect, done blowed his own brains out, and we went in there and destroyed evidence, triggering an Internal Affairs investigation ..."

"To be fair, sir, I didn't destroy the evidence. I wasn't even at the scene."

"It's your damn investigation, Latty. You decided Chapel was the bad guy!" White shouted. "This is going to come down hard on all of us, you most of all! You better keep the damn lid on this Hurst situation. We can't have any more screw-ups!"

"Well, sir, I'm afraid I have a little more bad news," Latty said. "We got results back on the packaging of the yellow rose and the prints on the dashboard. Looks like Shelton was in the car, sir."

"Tell me we can tie Shelton to Chapel?"

"I don't know how, sir. It's a stretch, and it flies in the face of our 'desperation robbery by a roid-raging Chapel theory."

"Well, Latty," White said slowly, "You've gone and gotten yourself in a real pickle. Either Michael Harold Chapel murdered Ms. Emogene Thompson, or YOU and your detectives done murdered him. Looks like you need to figure out which."

The bad news continued to pile up for Latty and the prosecution team. A lynchpin to their initial theory disintegrated. The allegations that Chapel had connections to the WBAC, the metro area criminal cops who had been grabbing headlines for the last two months due to a steroid and amphetamine-induced deadly crime spree, had no merit. Extensive testing and chemical analysis of his blood and urine conclusively revealed that fitness guru and Schwarzenegger look-a-like, Michael Chapel, was all-natural. He had no traces of steroids, amphetamines, blockers, or any other controlled substances in his bloodstream. Michael Chapel, it seems, followed his own advice where health and bodybuilding were concerned.

But the department was soon handed a major break in the case. A call came into GCPD in December 1993 from the General Manager of the American Inn, a woman named Delores. Delores reported that one of her employees, Tim Marco, had found a .38 caliber revolver lying in the mud next to the dumpster area on the hotel's property. Marco picked up the gun with a stick, examined it, noted the make of the weapon and two empty chambers. He also pointed out that the gun appeared to have started rusting slightly in some areas. Marco placed the gun in a plastic bag, carried it into the hotel, and placed it on the front desk.

A short while later, uniformed GCPD officer Tim Plunkett arrived at the American Inn. He examined the weapon in the plastic bag, then radioed someone on his shoulder-mounted mic. About ten minutes later, a senior police officer arrived in a late model Gwinnett County Police Car. He and Plunkett spoke for a few minutes outside the hotel; then Plunkett returned to the front desk.

Plunkett took the weapon and put it in the trunk of his squad car. He then picked up what appeared to be a red cloth or towel, wiped down the gun, returned it to its plastic bag, and dropped it in his trunk. Both officers got into their patrol cars and drove away.

Tim Marco, Delores, and another employee were perplexed by what they witnessed. Both suspected that the weapon found might be connected to Emogene Thompson, whose murder was widely discussed among the hotel staff.

Those at American Inn remembered Ms. Thompson well. She and her deceased boyfriend had been regular card players and gamblers on the premises. They also knew the victim's son, Michael Thompson, a frequent flyer at the motel. He spent time there shortly after the murder and as recently as four days before the gun was discovered.

Nine

Tim Marco felt the need to tell someone about the two police officers and Michael Thompson's recent stay at the American Inn. He learned from an article in the *Atlanta Journal Constitution* that Michael Chapel's defense attorney was Walt Britt. He found Britt's number in the yellow pages and called his office.

"Mr. Britt, this is Tim Marco. I work at the American Inn in Buford and was wondering if you'd heard anything from the Gwinnett County Police about finding the gun that possibly killed Emogene Thompson?"

Britt gave Tim Marco his full attention. "Well, no, Mr. Marco, I haven't heard that at all. Have you heard anything about Gwinnett Police finding the gun that possibly killed Emogene Thompson?"

Marco told his story. Britt sent a private investigator to get a detailed statement from Marco. The investigator surveyed the area where the gun was found, verified Marco's story with Delores, and off the record, asked his GCPD contacts what they knew.

The Investigator reported to Britt that he believed Marco's story was accurate. Britt sent several requests to Danny Porter asking about weapons found or obtained by GCPD since April 1993. It would take multiple requests, and Britt had to become explicit about the details, but Porter eventually acknowledged that GCPD had found the gun. Still, he could not make it available for testing because GCPD had the gun illegally destroyed twelve days after taking possession of it.

Chief of Detectives John Latty would later testify that he looked at the gun once and determined that it had no evidentiary value. Shortly thereafter, it was incinerated.

 **Ten**

"*There are alibis,*" *District Attorney Porter said* to Latty and Burnette, "And then there are iron-clad alibis. How can I place Michael Chapel at the scene when he can say, and I quote, 'I was standing in the firehouse with my shift commander, my watch partner, and a half dozen firemen while talking to dispatch and a police detective on the chronologically recorded police radio with the firehouse speaker squawking into my microphone from fourteen inches away!'"

"Yeah, but Reddy says..." Burnette began, but Porter ran over him.

"How can I place Chapel at the murder scene if he was miles away, fraternizing with half of Gwinnett County's first responders? Your case is coming apart!"

"I'm leaning on Stone," Burnette said again, spitting into a trash can. "We got ole Reddy's statement that he left at 2130. And after we reprimanded Rooster for sluffin' off at the firehouse, he's startin' to come around."

"I don't give a shit about what Rooster or Reddy say. When the jury hears these recordings, we might as well turn in our resignations and get measured for orange jumpsuits," Porter barked. "Don't you two get it? This tape will destroy us, for the love of God!"

"I'm so sorry, Mr. Porter, but I seem to have misplaced those recordings."

Porter stopped short and stared at Latty, who showed palms up.

"I've looked everywhere I can think of, and they are, unfortunately, just lost, sir." Latty looked at Porter with a confessional expression mixed with pride.

Porter's eyes shifted. He looked at Burnette, then back at Latty. With a lowered voice, he said, "Well, that is unfortunate." He snapped a rubber band around the tapes and tucked them in the bottom of the cardboard box marked '93-B 1818 Michael Chapel.' They would remain undisturbed for the next seventeen years.

"What about the firemen?" Burnette asked. "I understand a few of them done complained to their chief 'cause PD ain't been over there to take their statements."

"And what do you suppose they'll say if we trot on over there and put their statements on the record?" Latty lashed at Burnette.

"We could lean on 'em a little," Burnette said hesitantly, "like we're doing at PD."

"How's that work, Jack?" Porter snipped, "Your fat ass moseys on over to Fourteen trying to cajole half of Chief Hunnicutt's house, and he's going to sit back and shrug?"

"I reckon not, sir," Burnette said and spat into the trash can. "Any idears?"

"We're just going to have to slow-roll the firemen, stretch'em out, hope we get enough conflicting testimony at trial to muddy the waters," Porter said. "But on to another problem. I need something tying Chapel physically to the scene. The raincoat isn't going to do it. There appears to be human blood present, but nothing worth testing, and we are negative for gunpowder. I'll make a fuss over it, but Britt will bring in experts to destroy our analysis. I need Chapel's fingerprint on her car or her blood in his car, that kind of thing, something tangible. Anything?"

"We'll see what we can find, sir," Latty promised. Once Latty and Bur-nette returned to headquarters, Steve Cline was briefed on the meeting with the District Attorney and went to work on rebuilding the deflated case against Chapel. "Go back and recheck the front seat area of unit 197," Cline directed CSI technicians White and Jenkins. "Especially the armrest. Run another luminol test and see if you can find anything."

The watch officer looked for Chapel's inactivated patrol car on the se-cured PD impound yard's inventory list. "It's not here," he said. "It was never checked into impound."

Mary Ann White was confused. "Cline said it was brought here after we searched it, on the day they arrested Chapel; said he'd noticed suspicious smudges on the armrest we must've missed?"

"Y'all searched it out in front of HQ, right? It must still be up there," the watch officer guessed.

The techs carried their tool kits back through headquarters and out the main entrance, where they found unit 197 backed into a spot on the street side of the lot, near one of the large, twisted oaks. The unit was in the exact location as when Officer Chapel's wife, Eren, arrived at head-quarters seven days earlier, looking for her husband and right where it had been the first time these two techs searched the vehicle.

"Should they leave a subject vehicle out here unsecured?" Jenkins asked her partner.

"No," White said as she opened the driver's door, "and I'm pretty sure it shouldn't be unlocked, either."

The techs sprayed the front seat area with the luminol solution, as instructed by Sergeant Cline. Like magic, a small area near the front of the top of the arm rest that was in the down position luminesced. The fluorescent blue hue revealed the presence of approximately 40 nano-grams of human blood. The vehicle was then moved to the secured lot behind HQ and finally entered as evidence, control number 1741 at 1200, April 30, 1993.

The Georgia Bureau of Investigation crime lab would determine by five-point DNA testing, a new and soon to be proven unreliable method, that the blood matched the DNA profile of Emogene Thompson.

"Fantastic!" Porter exclaimed to the three men sitting at the conference table. "Now, we can inextricably link Mr. Robocop to this murder. I'm going to seek the death penalty."

"Now you're talkin'," said Latty.

"But we still need to establish that Chapel set up the meeting. Have we made any progress with the girlfriends?"

"Not really, sir," Latty reported. "Burel says she talked to Emogene like eight to ten times a day, and she expected Chapel to call and set a meeting, but nobody actually knows when or if that call was ever made."

"One of my ADAs pulled the phone records for the precinct, the gym, Chapel's residence, Thompson's residence, and Emogene's place of employment," Porter said. He added confidently, "We're examining them now, as is Lt. Powell and his bunch at I. A. We'll make the connection."

"The death penalty, sir?" Burnette circled back, still shocked that the District Attorney was considering capital punishment, "Are y'all sure we want, well....? Are y'all sure we wanna go down that road?"

"Well, Jack," Porter thundered, "It was a heinous crime and a wanton betrayal of the public's trust in law enforcement. It's a black mark on all of us who seek to protect and serve the citizens of Gwinnett County. He deserves to die for this crime!"

"But sir, we... well, I just didn't think we was talkin' about having the guy executed?"

"Listen, Jack," Latty interjected, "I know you considered Chapel a friend, and it's hard to see a friend and Brother in Blue fall so hard. But it boils down to the punishment fitting the crime. Either he committed this crime, and the DA needs to seek righteous judgment, or somebody else killed Emogene Thompson, and we all have hell to pay. It's not a hard decision for me. I'm with the DA on this."

Porter added, "I guess you just have to ask yourself if you believe in your own detective work and that of your colleagues. You, Latty, Cline, Ervin—you guys put in the work and cracked the case. Now you just have to give me enough evidence to secure a conviction. And the law says that conviction, with these circumstances, is a capital offense. Who are we to stand in the way of justice?"

"Justice," Burnette repeated quietly, while he slowly nodded his head then spit in the trash can.

"Yes, justice." Latty proclaimed, "That arrogant somebitch always thought he was some kinda super cop, untouchable. Well, we've got his ass in the hole, and he ain't coming out alive if I have anything to say about it."

"And thanks to your excellent detective work, Jack." Porter finished, "you and Cline finding the blood on the front seat of his patrol car where Emogene Thompson's stolen bloody purse undoubtedly deposited it after Chapel murdered her in cold blood! Our community and the Thompson family can get the justice we all deserve!"

Indeed, GCPD's detectives were able to rebuild a case against Chapel where the initial investigation had fallen apart. Numerous witnesses would contradict their own statements when testifying. Some of those witnesses have come forward to say that they were coerced by the police and coached by the District Attorney's office.

One witness, nineteen at the time of the murder, likened her interaction with the District Attorney's office as being stalked. "They demanded that I make a positive identification of Michael Chapel, even though it would have been impossible under the circumstances."

When this witness refused several different Assistant District Attorneys, she reports that Danny Porter himself showed up at her place of employment and tried to convince her that Chapel was guilty of several other crimes, so 'it was okay to positively identify him.' Recounting the experience brought her to tears some twenty-five years after the trial.

GCPD used an Internal Investigation to lean on officers, supervisors, and civilian employees. The department demanded that the name Michael

Chapel not be spoken amongst department employees regardless of rank. Those stepping out of line or defending Chapel were threatened or cajoled into acceptance and silence. In some cases, Danny Porter corresponded personally to threaten county employees.

One such civilian employee, who remains a Gwinnett County employee hired an attorney to demand GCPD cease and desist all harassment and threatening behavior.

Chapel's immediate supervisor, D. E. Stone, and his watch partner, Reddy, both have Chapel, ironically, as their alibi for the night of the murder but would change their own stories multiple times to fit Porter's narrative. Both were disciplined and faced further action by the department, and both ultimately testified for the prosecution.

In total, sixty-one officers were demoted, suspended, or internally disciplined in connection with the Northside Internal Investigation. The 100-page report produced by that investigation has not been released to the public and has remained sealed since it was completed twenty-seven years ago.

Like the Michael Chapel investigation, it was conducted by GCPD, in direct violation of the Commission on Accreditation for Law Enforcement Agencies (*CALEA*) guidelines, which certified their accreditation as a Police Department.

In most cases, standard protocol requires law enforcement agencies to turn over conflicted investigations, such as officer-involved shootings, to outside agencies such as the Georgia Bureau of Investigation or the FBI.

GCPD achieved its accreditation from CALEA in 1993, affirming that it did meet and would follow the organization's requirements and guidelines. Considering the Michael Chapel Investigation that started in mid-April 1993 and the internal investigation of the Northside Precinct that began shortly after that, it begs the question: Did GCPD ever meet accreditation requirements, or has the Gwinnett County Police Department operated as a rogue police force for all these many years?

Eleven

"*Walt Britt has got to go!*" Danny Porter said to County Attorney John Underwood. "His discovery requests are killing me, and he knows that PD had the Keystone Cops investigating this murder. He is going to destroy us at trial."

"Calm down, Danny," said Underwood, the County's top civil litigator, and contracts expert. A graduate of Georgia Tech and the Georgia State College of Law, also a former Associate Editor of the Georgia State Law Review.

"Don't tell me to calm down! Nothing Latty and his fat-ass sidekick presented pre-arraignment has held up. The prosecution witnesses are all over the map. Their prime suspect's alibi is strong, motive is weak, and they've destroyed or lost more evidence than Georgia has peach trees."

"Have you considered dropping the charges, Danny?" Underwood asked bluntly.

"Yeah? How would that go?" Porter asked caustically. "Oops, sorry, Officer Chapel, we just learned that our investigative team is dumb as hell after we accused you of murder, arraigned you, and told the press, the Judge, God, and everybody else that you, sir, are a grandma-murdering degenerate. We held you in solitary confinement for the last six months while we destroyed your reputation, your career, and your family, but now, hey, you're free to go. No hard feelings!"

"Just a thought."

"Another thought! I don't know for sure if we would go to jail, but I'm quite sure he'd own Gwinnett. And I doubt Chapel County would have a position open for a county attorney that stripped him of his job and pension or a one-term DA that pressed the charges. So, no John, no, I haven't considered dropping the charges!"

Underwood ignored the sarcasm. "Then have you thought about having his hippy attorney conflicted out? Britt represents the county in a number of matters. Maybe the Judge would give him the boot?"

"We talked about that with the Judge before arraignment. Bishop didn't think it was a big deal. None of Britt's work for the County has anything to do with PD, and he has defended other cops while also working for the county."

"Hear me out," said Underwood. "With the decision coming up for the County Commissioners, on Chapel's employment, I could make a stink about it and try to get the issue in front of the press. Then you could use that to get it back in front of Bishop. If he takes up the issue, I'll brief it from the County's perspective, and you can attack the conflict. What do you think?"

"It's worth a shot," Porter said. "I can't have that hippy boy picking apart my case. He's already done enough damage—not as much as GCPD— but we haven't even gotten through discovery yet!"

Underwood and Porter began stirring the pot concerning the upcoming employment decision and whether there was a general conflict of interest in what the press called Britt's part-time representation of some of the county's municipal organizations. That representation included the city of Buford, which was expected to produce several government employees to testify at the upcoming trial. As 1993 raced toward 1994, the issue heated up.

Britt was no stranger to conflict allegations. He successfully argued in a number of cases that relationships with an employer or even familial relationships do not automatically constitute a conflict, citing a case he lost with two cousins on the jury. Relationships don't necessarily create prejudice or conflict, but believing Bishop would stand by his earlier position, Britt filed a preemptive motion on October 5, 1993, requesting the Judge rule as to whether or not Britt should be conflicted out.

He was not expecting an immediate response from the County's top attorneys, but both Underwood and Porter pounced on the issue and filed briefs asking the Judge to remove Britt and appoint new counsel.

Underwood argued that Britt represented the county in fourteen cases, and it would be unfair to force the county to hire new attorneys while Britt was tied up with the Chapel case. Meanwhile, Porter focused on the conflict angle, citing Chapel's employment by the county. He also asserted that the case was not so complex that new counsel would find it difficult to get up to speed quickly.

Officer Chapel was officially fired from GCPD on October 9, 1993, and the Honorable Judge Fred Bishop disqualified Walt Britt as Michael Chapel's attorney on November 24. Britt immediately appealed to the Georgia Supreme Court and was quoted in the *Atlanta Journal-Constitution*, "I fail to see how the county or the state have demonstrated sufficient conflict in a timely manner to cause the defendant to lose the counsel of his choice. It is my opinion that the trial court abused its discretion."

Britt also made an issue regarding the budget allocated to the defense in the trial. He was now working through the Public Defender's Statute appointed by the judge since the Chapels ran out of money to pay for his defense.

"This is preposterous, Your Honor!" Britt argued in the closed hearing in early January 1994, before the Supreme Court opinion came down. He wore his signature jeans and a blue suede blazer, his salt and pepper hair pulled into a ponytail, "The prosecution is estimating close to $400,000 in expenditures for this public railroad, and all you can allocate for defense investigative services is $2,000? That's a damn joke. This man is fighting for his life, and you'll have him fighting blindfolded with both hands tied behind his back."

"I'm going to have to ask you to watch your tone, Mr. Britt. This Court will be addressed respectfully."

"I'll watch my tone when the Court stops allowing my esteemed colleague over there and the Court itself to run roughshod over my client's civil rights, Your Honor." Britt snapped back at the Judge.

"You're dancing dangerously close to contempt, counsel!" The Judge warned.

"I'm well past contempt, Your Honor. The Court, respectfully, has lost its mind. You are conflicting me out of this matter because my good friend," Britt pointed at the District Attorney Danny Porter, who stared at the yellow legal pad in front of him. "Mr. Porter over there knows he has a pitiful case, and he knows I have access to the facts and files to get to the bottom of it. He wants you to appoint some Public Defender flunky who doesn't have a snowball's chance in hell of derailing this out-of-control train wreck headed straight for my client!"

"Bailiff!" Judge Bishop summoned.

Britt was sentenced to three days of incarceration and booked into the county jail. A clerk came from the courthouse two hours later to relay a message from Judge Bishop. "Apologize to the court, and the contempt charge and sentence will be dropped." Britt informed the clerk to let the Judge know he could "go piss up a rope." Britt spent the entire seventy-two hours in jail.

Shortly after that, Officer Chapel had a new lead defense attorney, Johnny R. Moore. Mr. Moore, a Georgia State and Emory Law School Graduate left the Gwinnett County District Attorney's office in 1984. He and Danny Porter had worked there together.

It is believed that Moore hired Porter as an assistant district attorney and supervised him for a time. Moore had tried two murder cases; both resulted in life sentences for his client. Judge Bishop appointed Moore and a young public defender, Elizabeth Vila Rogan, as co-counsel. Porter had successfully insulated himself and the Chapel case from Walt Britt. He was pleased.

 **Twelve**

Karl Kautter looked at police lineup photo #38. Kautter was a passenger in the car driven by Paul Omodt on April 15, 1993, and was now a reluctant witness for the prosecution.

"That's not J. P. Morgan," Kautter said, startling Porter, who had not mentioned Morgan and expected his key eyewitness to identify Chapel.

Omodt reported seeing a six-foot-tall police officer wearing a yellow rain slicker and a yellow smokie-style police hat. He was carrying an engaged flashlight in his right hand and was walking to the dark-colored sedan parked in front of the police car. The blue lights atop the police vehicle flashed as they crested the hill but were off when they passed the scene.

Kautter himself had some history with both GCPD officers J. P. Morgan and Michael Chapel. He would say in court that he had never met Chapel, which the records prove false. Chapel had issued him a traffic citation D27121in 1988, which Kautter disputed in court. That dispute meant that Chapel was required to be present for the court appearance.

Moreover, Chapel had months earlier surveilled a suspected chop shop off Peachtree Industrial Boulevard, owned and operated by Mr. Kautter. Shortly after that surveillance, Officer Chapel walked in on Officer J. P. Morgan rifling through his confidential intel files. The files, located in precinct commander Captain Cantrell's office, included investigative details on the alleged Kautter chop shop and confidential informant reports on Morgan's dealings with Tookie and his drug trafficking ring and other nefarious activities.

Captain Cantrell, seemingly embarrassed by the expose, offered that he was assisting Morgan locate a bad guy.

Dissatisfied with the excuse and given the adversarial relationship between Chapel and Morgan, Chapel contacted Narcotics Sergeant Billy Carty, his confidant, and liaison for the narcotics cases. Carty and Chapel decided to relocate the files from Cantrell's office to a more secure place.

On the day the files were relocated, Chapel arrived at the precinct earlier than usual. He prepared for patrol duty, proceeded to roll call, then removed the files from Cantrell's office. The files were placed in two lockers in an unused part of the locker room, where they remained padlocked until after Chapel's arrest.

Once Chapel was in custody, the lockers were forced open, the files taken into GCPD custody, and subsequently 'lost,' like so much other evidence, before the trial began in 1995.

Morgan purportedly had dealings with Kautter on a more personal level. According to Morgan's handyman, Kautter's business provided Renee Morgan with a shiny, late model BMW. The handyman-maintained Morgan's rental properties. Mrs. Morgan called this handyman to clear out and clean up the 'death-room' after J. P. Morgan's suicide.

It must also be considered that Morgan, like approximately 90% of the GCPD, fit the description often repeated by several witnesses, including Kautter and Omodt. A medium-built, dark-haired white male, approximately six feet tall. A Grand Canyon-sized chasm of difference exists between that description and a six-foot-seven-inch man weighing in at nearly 290 pounds.

If these witnesses had seen Michael Chapel—in tactical boots, smokie hat, and size 6X yellow rain slicker—towering nearly thirty inches above the dark-colored sedan, they would have described Big Foot in a Big Bird costume, not an average cop.

Twelve

Later, Kautter admitted he was pressured by GCPD and schooled by ADA Tom Davis on what to say and how to say it. He would, however, point the identifying finger at photo #38, Michael Chapel, and state, *"I'll have to say that is him."*

Kautter's entire testimony can only be described as a string of lies.

Interestingly, Kautter emphatically stated that he was not sworn in as he gave his testimony. He later reached out to Johnny Moore and admitted to a number of his lies. Allegedly threatened with a perjury charge by Danny Porter if he were to recant his testimony, Kautter sought immunity from prosecution through his attorney.

In 1993, Kautter had claimed to be a passenger traveling northbound on Peachtree Industrial Boulevard when they passed Gwinnco Muffler Shop. He noted the six-foot, medium-built policeman with a flashlight, walking up to the dark-colored sedan parked in front of the Gwinnett County Police car.

As Kautter and the driver proceeded northbound to the point where the two-lane expands to four, he noticed a police car pulling alongside them. This car, allegedly the same Gwinnett County police car they had just passed, would travel alongside them for forty-five seconds, with the inside overhead light on, allowing Kautter to make eye contact with and positively identify Michael Chapel.

He made the ID after he noted, without prompting, that the man highlighted in the lineup, whom he knew GCPD wanted him to pick was not J. P. Morgan. Morgan was not included in the photo lineup nor were any other Northside officers. The identification confusion is not the only troubling part of Kautter's testimony.

A simple mathematical impossibility exists between the time the officer in the smokie hat was seen and the time he pulled past the car in which Kautter was a passenger.

In order for the officer to return to his vehicle, presumably after firing the two fatal shots, which Kautter and Omodt did not hear, back the patrol car out onto Peachtree Industrial Boulevard, catch up to the two men and ride alongside them for nearly forty-five seconds before making the first right past Highway 20 a mere seven-tenths of a mile from the driveway to the muffler shop, the officer would have been traveling at roughly 200 miles per hour.

In 2011, when speaking to Private Investigator Pamela Holcombe, Kautter said, "Mike Chapel got a raw deal." He told Holcombe that the DA's office had pressured him to testify and coached him on what to say. He was also instructed to lie about his drinking.

On the night in question, Kautter was told not to mention or admit that he had been drinking and doing drugs at a BMW dealership gala. He and Omodt were on their way home from there when they passed the muffler shop. Moreover, he claimed he was drinking at lunch, just before taking the witness stand as Porter's only eyewitness tying Chapel to the scene. Facts of his excessive drinking and self-described drug addictions were allegedly known to the District Attorney. These facts were reportedly covered up with assistance from Porter's office.

Holcombe asked Kautter if he believed Michael Chapel was the cop he saw that night and if he thought Chapel killed Emogene Thompson. His response: "J. P. Morgan was the shooter. Mike Chapel got railroaded."

"You look like you've been run over by a train, baby," Michael Chapel said to his usually vibrant and cheerful wife.

In the lead-up to the trial, Chapel was held at the Gwinnett County lock-up.

"Same train, honey!" his beleaguered bride responded. "It's so crazy. All the horrible things they are saying, Mike. I know none of it is true, but I just don't understand how these men can say these things about you. They know it's not true! Jack, and Rooster, Billy Carty?"

"I know, babe."

"And Danny Porter can't find enough TV cameras to call you a cold-blooded killer. He's all, 'why else would he have sounded so calm?' Gee, I don't know Danny. Maybe he was calm because he didn't do anything! And why should we just take Latty's word for it? Where are

Twelve

the tapes?"

"Well, honey," Michael said with purposeful calm, "Danny Porter slid all his chips to the middle of the table when he charged me with murder. He's playing his hand out now, no matter the cards he's holding."

"It can't be that simple, Mike, can it?" Eren swiped her forehead with a shaking hand. "It can't be that he is willing to send an innocent man to the electric chair because Latty had a hunch? It can't be that Danny Porter is simply unwilling to admit that he was wrong?"

"As hard as it is to believe, honey," Mike somberly replied, "I'm afraid it is that simple. John Latty has failed so many times that a case like this would end his career for him to get it wrong. Same with Porter, this is his first term, I'm not sure he'd be willing to admit that he was wrong regardless, but to do so now, he wouldn't have a second term."

Thirteen

"No, ma'am," *Danny Porter said defiantly* to the 78-year-old citizen, "I won't be apologizing to your grandson. Just because the jury found him not guilty doesn't mean he's innocent."

"But the State's Chief Medical Examiner testified and told you personally that the poor little girl died from the brain clot!" Alice Weeks voice wavered. "Bless her soul, she had that clot weeks before my grandson babysat for her, and your own medical examiner agreed with the State's Medical Examiner that there had been no signs of sexual assault. Yet, you spent the last two years on every TV screen in Georgia calling my sweet little grandson a rapist and baby killer. But you don't think you owe him an apology, sir?"

"Well, ma'am," Porter said, "It doesn't much matter to me what the Medical Examiner thinks. I had a case, so I made it. That's my job. The jury acquitted him, so that's the end of it, but I stand by my case."

And so ended the prosecution of then fourteen-year-old Christopher Routh for the sexual assault and murder of twenty-three-month-old Emily Woodruff, whom he was babysitting when she stopped breathing on July 25, 2001, in her parent's Loganville home.

Emily had been to the emergency room a week earlier with what was thought to be a stomach virus and laborious breathing. The radiologist did a complete work-up of x-rays and somehow missed the clot forming in her brain.

The child was treated for a spleen disorder and prescribed medication that her parents failed to purchase. For most of her life, the child had also been suffering from eczema, causing her to scratch herself around the area that led GCPD detective Matt Marshall to determine the child had been sexually assaulted.

Once John Latty listened to the 911 call made by Routh, he described the fourteen-year-old in precisely the same manner he had described Officer Michael Chapel nearly a decade prior: 'calm and collected, the demeanor of a cold-blooded killer!'

As he had in 1993, Danny Porter would take up that mantra—'The demeanor of a cold-blooded killer'—and brand Christopher Routh in the court of public opinion before trying to poison the jury with the same speculation.

As with the case the *State of Georgia v. Michael Harold Chapel*, there was another perfectly reasonable explanation for the apparently calm and collected demeanor of the boy calling 911 for help, and later, while being questioned by Homicide Detectives.

Christopher had been taught from a young age while learning to scuba dive, 'you panic, you die.' Routh's unflappable father, Charlie, an accomplished diver raised in Alaska, taught young Christopher that overreaction and panic are common ingredients for lives short-lived.

GCPD was not impressed and decided early on they were dealing with a heartless murderer. The public demanded that someone be held to account for this unthinkable act, and Danny Porter relished his second fifteen minutes of fame, surely it would catapult him to higher office.

As had happened in the lead up to the 1995 *State v. Chapel*, the airtight case brought to the District Attorney by GCPD began to deteriorate. GCPD insisted the swelling in the young girl's brain was caused by 'Shaken Baby Syndrome,' even without other bruising expected in such cases. The x-rays told another story. Those x-rays were inexplicably 'lost.'

Witness testimony was manipulated. Without the benefit of a complete diagnosis, first responders and medical assistants were called to point the finger at Routh. Routh was the kid that virtually anyone with a television in the State of Georgia had heard referred to as a 'cold-blooded baby killer.'

Instead of stepping back to take a harder look at the facts in front of them, Porter and GCPD would go to work throwing more hot coals on the engine burner, no matter where they had to shovel the coal from, and no matter whose rights they would need to violate to fan the flames. Once the *Gwinnett County Railroad* left the station, it was conviction at all costs.

Shortly after the warrant was issued for Christopher's arrest, Charlie Routh dropped his ten-year-old daughter, Emily, off at her Grandparent's home while he tended to the matters at hand with his son, who was at that moment a fugitive. GCPD officers accompanied by two homicide detectives descended on the Week's residence.

While an officer and one of the detectives searched the home for Christopher, commanding the 82-year-old disabled veteran grandfather's attention, they questioned Alice weeks about the whereabouts of the couple's grandson. The other detective happened upon Emily in the open garage. She had gone outside to retrieve some toys just before GCPD's arrival.

After several minutes passed, Alice Weeks went looking for her granddaughter when the child did not return to the playroom. She found Emily sitting in a child's folding chair, crying. The GCPD detective and uniformed officer alleged that her brother must be abusing her, too, and interrogated her as to her brother's whereabouts.

As he had done in the Chapel case, Porter tried to negotiate an interruption-free summation so he could leave the jury with his version of the case. Routh's Attorney, Doug Peters, an able and reputable defense attorney, would not hear of it. Unlike Johnny Moore in the Chapel case, Peters and his co-counsel, Phillis Miller, would hold Porter's feet to his own fire.

With the testimony from the medical examiners, including the State of Georgia's Chief M. E. Kris Sperry appearing, for the first and only time in his career, for the defense, it took the jury only a few hours to deliberate and acquitted Routh on all charges.

"There was no proof to convict him," Jury foreman Bruce Griffin would say following the verdict.

Charlie and Sissy were ecstatic to have their son home, though they would always contend that the ordeal stole their son's childhood.

"He went to jail a boy; he came back a man." Charlie would say, "And really, the whole family was changed forever."

Little Emily would endure years of harassment. Classmates called her brother a baby killer and maligned her family. Like her brother, she harnessed a profound inner strength and drew closer to her family, including her calm, collected, accused, and acquitted big brother. She excelled academically and in sports, eventually earned a master's degree, and currently serves as the Head Soccer Coach at a Gwinnett County High School.

Charlie and Sissy endured the darkest of days and faced their deepest fears with unimaginable determination, faith, and love for their children.

Christopher returned to high school, faced scorn and ridicule despite exoneration, and held his head high with the same calm demeanor that had branded him a cold-blooded killer. He made the varsity football team, graduated in the top five of his class, went away to college on an academic scholarship, and earned a law degree. Eventually, he became a death-qualified public defender and has dedicated his life to defending those least fortunate among us and most in need of an advocate.

Chris learned as a teenager that those in power do not always play by the rules. Lady Justice, as they say, is blind. If those who administer justice do not care about truth and right, while facts are manipulated by the system, then that system can swallow any one of us at any time. Chris survived the *Gwinnett County Railroad* and became a great example of the legal profession despite his ignominious introduction to the law.

Another young man laid low on the tracks of the Gwinnett County Justice system was Quintrellis Head, a twenty-four-year-old father of three. Quintrellis and his wife, Akilah Denson, relocated their young family to

Norcross from Alabama in search of an opportunity in the post-Olympic boom town of *Hotlanta*. Another deciding factor in the family's migration was the proximity to Emory's world-renowned cardiology center. Takitre Yanise Head, nicknamed Beenie by the family, was often treated there.

Beenie, a premature baby, weighed less than two pounds at birth. She was diagnosed with cardiomyopathy, sickle cell anemia, and other serious medical conditions.

When the child stopped breathing on May 5, 2001, her father, Quintrellis, called 911 and frantically performed CPR on his frail and dying child. He could not revive little Beenie, and when two Gwinnett County Detectives interrogated him, he could not articulate the litany of Beenie's medical challenges and diagnoses.

By the time Akilah returned home from the hair salon and learned of her daughter's passing, her distraught husband was a suspect and her living room a crime scene.

How had this happened?

GCPD Major Steve Cline was concerned with scratches around Beenie's mouth, a swollen lip, and a bruise on her head. Cline was skeptical when the injuries were explained as the result of a fall on the concrete steps outside their apartment a few days earlier and an allergic reaction to the medication prescribed at the hospital. He suspected the injuries were signs of abuse.

But the fall had occurred when Beenie was chasing her older sister, Akitre, in a game of tag. Multiple adult neighbors witnessed the fall, and the child was immediately taken to the Gwinnett Medical Center and treated.

GCPD interviewed none of the witnesses on the scene or at the hospital. They reviewed none of the 500 pages of medical records from the Emory Clinic and the Alabama hospital where Beenie had been born.

After reviewing only, the emergency room report and examination of the deceased child, Forensic Investigator Jim Dempsey noted in his report,

"There is no readily apparent cause of death."

Once the report was forwarded to Gwinnett Chief Medical Examiner, Dr. Steven Dunton, an autopsy report was issued with a cause of death: "Blunt force trauma to the head, not explained by the fall onto concrete steps."

ADA Tom Davis fired up the *Gwinnett County Railroad*. Felony murder and first-degree child endangerment trains went racing down the tracks.

Several weeks later, Quintrellis went to Detroit to attend a long-planned family reunion when Danny Porter notified the press that GCPD was engaged in a manhunt for Head, who was now officially charged for the murder of his child.

"Quintrellis Head was never running from the law," explained Head's attorney, Tee Okonkwo. Once the accused heard the reports of the warrant being issued for his arrest, he immediately returned to Georgia and turned himself in.

Okonkwo's tenacity would eventually force the District Attorney's office to review the medical records. Once a Broward County Medical Examiner was ordered to reexamine the case, Dr. Dunton changed the cause of death. Conclusion: Beenie died of natural causes.

Porter had no choice but to drop all charges against Quintrellis Head, who by then had spent seventeen months in jail awaiting his constitutionally guaranteed speedy trial.

Upon Head's release, his mother, Janise Odom, lashed out at Porter and Dunton. "They put his face on every TV channel and hunted him down like a common criminal while we were on a family vacation…I want to tell them just to tell the truth. You made a mistake!" Mrs. Odom said.

The DA's response was classic Porter: "Innocence means he didn't do it. Dropping the charges just means we can't prove he did it."

Over the years, on many occasions, Danny Porter would be accused of overzealous prosecution. His reputation as a publicity hound is well documented. Any opportunity to admit his error, or on the part of his

Thirteen

staff or Gwinnett County Law Enforcement, was met with denial and dismissal.

At one point, Danny Porter noted that the Quintrellis Head case was the only murder charge his office had ever dropped. The pattern seems clear upon examination, particularly in high-profile cases—sloppy detective work, pressure from the press and the public, and a rush to judgment by the District Attorney's office. When a case begins to fall apart, then conviction by all means necessary becomes the rule of engagement. The Constitution and the rule of law be damned.

Once a defendant is charged, the *Gwinnett County Railroad* races down the tracks with no U-turn possible, and it all started with Danny Porter's first big case: *The State of Georgia v. Michael Harold Chapel*.

Fourteen

Chapel's new defense team, approved by Danny Porter and appointed by Judge Fred Bishop, decided to take a pretrial field trip to GBI Headquarters on Panthersville Road, Decatur, Georgia. The purpose of this trip was to examine the state's evidence being tested by the GBI and stored at the state's primary crime lab.

Johnny Moore, Elizabeth Rogan, Defense Investigator Dennis Miller, and Dr. Reese, a hired Serologist, met representatives from the DA's office and Dr. Keith Goff, head of the GBI's DNA Testing programs. The defense team was taken on a brief tour of the facility that culminated in the testing lab, where the evidence in GBI custody was observed.

There was a wood table with roughly fourteen square feet of the surface. There were what appeared to be evidentiary items and a few note pads on its surface. Dr. Goff cleared a spot on the table, removed Emogene Thompson's clothing from unsealed plastic evidence bags, and spread them out, one by one, on the work surface.

Curiously, Dr. Goff did not wear gloves throughout, even though there were numerous boxes of sterile latex gloves around the lab. To the astonishment of the defense team, Dr. Goff made no attempt to wipe down the wooden surface between articles. By the time he returned the crime scene evidence to their bags, visible accumulations of dried blood had flaked off onto the tabletop's porous surface.

Michael Chapel

As the defense attorneys discussed the matter with Dr. Reese, Investigator Miller snapped photos and shot a video documenting the contaminated surface. While the attorneys were discussing what course of action, if any, they needed to undertake, Dr. Goff walked out of the Lab's freezer holding an unsealed green igloo cooler.

He set it down and began to remove its contents, stacking each item on the edge of the worktop table. Before lead attorney Johnny Moore collected thoughts, Dr. Goff picked up the top item on the stack. It was the first item placed in the cooler when it was taken into evidence by GCPD—Michael Chapel's size 6X, department-identified yellow raincoat.

He took hold of each shoulder and flipped the coat outward as if he were unfurling a sleeping bag in the woods. He then placed the rapidly thawing giant rain slicker onto the blood-contaminated table. The slicker covered most of the surface and still crinkled from being crammed inside the cooler. Dr. Goff used his ungloved hands that had not been washed since handling the victim's clothing. He smoothed the raincoat pressing it firmly onto the contaminated tabletop.

At this point, Dr. Reese told lead defense attorney, Johnny Moore, that the raincoat no longer had any evidentiary value. According to the serologist, the coat that tested negative for gunpowder but was not tested for DNA or blood typing, was now hopelessly contaminated.

The defense decided it was best just to document. Dr. Goff flipped the coat over, and once again, smoothed both sides. After pictures and video were taken of this raincoat contamination, the rain pants were handled in the same manner.

At no time did Goff wash his hands, wipe down the table between articles, or don protective hand covering while handling crucial evidence. Dr. Reese commented to the defense attorneys that it was hard enough to believe that Georgia's premier crime lab had such lax standards, but what they had just witnessed looked like evidence handling from the 1960s.

Johnny Moore was elated to hear the opinion that the raincoat would not be allowed into evidence. Thus, a considerable part of the prosecution's anticipated case was now a dead stick.

"Great news Mike!" Moore started the prisoner counselor session at Hall County Detention Center, "The raincoat is completely contaminated. Porter will never get it entered into evidence!"

"What the hell, Johnny?" Chapel raised his voice. "Do you believe that I killed Ms. Thompson, or are you just trying to help Porter kill me?"

"Mike, no, I don't understand," Moore said. "Of course, I believe you. I just thought getting Danny Porter's so-called blood-spatter evidence disqualified would help your defense."

"It would help my defense if I was guilty!" Chapel said. "I was not there that night, so the only way Emogene's blood would be on my raincoat is if they put it there, and it sounds like that's just what they did at the crime lab, whether intentional or not. You absolutely should have stopped that from occurring, and you should have been screaming bloody murder to get that raincoat tested for DNA before the contamination!" Concern for his future fell on Mike like the proverbial ton of bricks.

"I'm really sorry, Mike," the feeble attorney said. "I hadn't thought of it in that way. I was just caught off guard by the whole spectacle."

"I understand," Chapel said, controlling himself, "but please understand, I am on trial for my life here, and I am telling you the facts. If you don't believe me, or if you can't fight for an innocent man, then you need to get Judge Bishop to give me a lawyer who will."

Moore swore to Chapel he would fight for him, and he appeared to do so at times. But like many folks around Gwinnett County, it was hard for Johnny Moore to believe the police, or his friend and colleague, Danny Porter, would intentionally try to convict an innocent man, particularly in a death penalty case. Yet, a closer look at the grievous mishandling of evidence, in this case, seems beyond the point of statistical coincidence.

Start with evidence taken from the crime scene: the yellow rose in a clear plastic container on the dashboard of the victim's car. Neither the rose nor its container was properly logged into evidence and was not presented to the defense team as required by the U.S. Supreme Court (Brady v. Maryland). Further, it was never located. Copies of crime scene photos show that the rose existed, but these were withheld from the defense—another Brady violation—the withheld photos show the rose on the dashboard in plain sight during the initial canvas.

There can be little doubt that the rose packaging was tested for latent fingerprints. The evidence log that would have contained the rose was clearly altered or fabricated as it was signed four different times on the chain of custody section by Jack Burnette. It was signed with the same pen, ink pressure, and overlapping of other signatures.

Some of those signatures overlapped by Burnette's were dated after the date on Burnette's signature, meaning they should have overlapped Burnette's signature and not the other way around. Burnette's signatures, which according to handwriting experts, all occurred on the same day, were for a chain of custody that spanned over two and a half years.

Four fingerprints found in the front of the victim's vehicle, around the dash area, were described by a CSI technician as 'too small for an adult' and were allegedly discarded before they could be compared to local, state, or federal databases or examined by the defense.

The crime scene video turned over to the defense and played for the jury had been spliced down from three hours to a mere one minute and forty-three seconds, with many critical angles simply removed from the video presentation.

The flat tire was logged into evidence and said to have been slashed by a single edge blade, potentially as a cover-up by the killer. Upon closer examination of the reports initially filed in the case, Ed Byers, the responding officer, only noticed the cuts after the vehicle was moved for loading onto a flatbed wrecker.

Photos of the car resting on location at Gwinnco reveal that crime scene tape, which had been loosely placed around the vehicle to 'seal the scene,' blew onto the tire, coming to rest at the bottom where the rubber meets the road. The rest of the tire is visible and pristine. The cuts were not seen until the car was moved because the car rolled to a stop with the cuts at the very bottom of the tire. This action made it unlikely, if not impossible, for the slashes to have occurred at the muffler shop.

It would have been easy to test the tire to see if it had run-flat, yet this testing never occurred, and the cut-away sample of the tire, intended for use as evidence by the prosecution, was 'lost.'

The spare patrol car, the only vehicle in GCPD's inventory that matched the description, attested to by numerous witnesses, of the police car at the scene, was unavailable for defense examination and never officially subjected to forensic examination by GCPD.

Likewise, the victim's vehicle, the actual crime scene, was not available for defense examination and was not preserved by the prosecution, as mandated by state and federal law. The vehicle was released to the victim's son, who testified that the car was immediately sold to a person he could not remember for a forgotten amount of money.

When Chapel was interrogated by Lt. Latty and Jack Burnette, the man that called him-self Chapel's good friend, Chapel begged Burnette to ask the firemen for corroboration of his alibi. He asked Burnette to listen to the dispatch tapes for the truth—that Michael Chapel was at Firehouse Fourteen responding to dispatch on the chronologically recorded police dispatch radio, standing fourteen inches away from the chronologically recorded fire dispatch speakers. Burnette promised he would talk to the firemen and listen to the tapes. He said Chapel could 'take that to the bank.'

Lt. Latty listened to those tapes once and reported that Michael Chapel sounded calm and collected, 'like a cold-blooded killer,' and then 'lost' the recordings. It may be unclear if negligence can be considered a Brady violation. Still, since the tapes showed up 17 years later in an evidence box reviewed by a private investigator while in the possession and presence of District Attorney Danny Porter, it is hard to imagine how it could be otherwise.

A gun found at the American Inn matched the description of the subject's weapon, including the two empty chambers. This gun, a shrouded .38, was not subjected to standard police processing or rules of evidentiary procedure. The gun was taken into Gwinnett Police Department custody. Lt. John Latty declared it of no evidentiary value, and it was

promptly destroyed in an incinerator within twelve days. This all
occurred sixteen days after the victim's son, an initial suspect in the
Emogene Thompson murder, stayed at the hotel in close proximity to the
weapon. The weapon having been found four days after his stay.

Wheldon Seay, the gentlemen who bought the victim's trailer, found
a fired .38 caliber bullet behind Emogene Thompson's trailer, approximately 50 yards from where her purse was later found. Mr. Seay turned
this bullet over to GCPD, expecting that they would run ballistics. No
testing was done, and GCPD 'lost' the bullet.

Wheldon Seay also told Jack Burnette that he planted a recording device in the trailer where Amy Parker resided with his son, Keith. Seay
reported Amy Parker saying that in the days before the initial burglary at
Emogene Thompson's home, she and her baby daddy, Scooter Coggins,
could go into Emogene's trailer anytime they chose and steal her money.
Parker admitted to entering Emogene Thompson's trailer before she left
for work on the night of the murder, allegedly to use the phone. There
were no records of any phone calls in or out during that time frame.

The elder Seay explained his theory to Burnette. *"And I thought to myself,
well now, if somebody wanted to stick a tire, that'd be a good way to do it. Be
over there and just walk back and stick the tire, you know, to make the tire go
flat where she couldn't get around the corner very far, you know. So that's what
really started making me suspicious of her."*

At this point, Burnette had to know, as did the entire crime scene team
and the District Attorney's office, that the cuts in the tire were at the bottom of the tire and therefore not made at Gwinnco Muffler shop, which
is 1.6 miles from Emogene Thompson's driveway.

Yet, Burnette's response was, *"Yes, sir. I can put you at ease on that. The tire
was cut where the car was sitting."* (Gwinnco)

Seay seemed surprised but still voiced suspicions about Amy Parker. He
was told she knew Michael Chapel and insisted that Parker also knew
other police officers, and Seay was apprehensive about her possible relationship with Burnette.

"I'm a little bit leery about talking to you is the reason I'm saying that, because

she comes back, and she says some things to me that made me question whether or not you (Burnette) and her (Parker) were even friends?" Burnette denied knowing Parker beyond the interview with her in connection to the case.

Amy Parker had regular contact with another law enforcement officer: Marshall Chris Robertson, from Sugar Hill. Robertson was not the responding officer when Emogene Thompson's body was discovered but was the first law enforcement officer to arrive at Gwinnco Muffler Shop that morning.

Robertson, a one-time suspect, admitted to lying to GCPD about his contacts with Amy Parker and other members of her Sugar Hill Gang.

Burnette dismissed Robertson as a suspect because he was left-handed. Robertson did, however, fit the general description of the officer seen wearing a white shirt. The Marshall uniform consisted of a white collared shirt, and the his patrol car loosely fit the description of the boxy white police car. He is a white male with brown hair and approximately six feet tall. His alibi at the time of the murder is unknown.

Burnette seemed to want to steer Mr. Seay away from his suspicions and armchair investigation, or at least get him thinking the same way as the Police Investigation.

"Hold on a minute and let me put you at ease on this," said Burnette. *"I don't know that anybody other than Mike Chapel had any involvement in the murder."*

Burnette allowed Seay to believe that Chapel was possibly sleeping with Amy Parker and that he had been a dancer at the Lemon Peel, a nude review. Something Burnette, a close associate of Chapel, knew to be untrue.

When Seay asked if Chapel wrote up the initial call with the victim as a domestic call instead of a burglary and perhaps Parker told Chapel where the money was—things there was no evidence of whatsoever. Burnette answered.

"Yes, sir."

Mr. Seay offered his recordings to GCPD. He offered to gather more incriminating intel on Amy Parker and her Sugar Hill Gang, which included his son. He offered to facilitate an interview with his son, Keith.

Seay told Burnette when and how his niece, Becky Seay, a Dixie-Mafia connected drug pusher, would show up at Amy Parker's place three or four times a month. These visits, often coinciding with the arrival of Amy Parker's welfare checks, were for drug distribution. Like clockwork, her customers arrived shortly after Becky, stayed a while, and left as the next group of customers arrived.

Seay also explained to Burnette that Parker had divulged information about a safe-cracking ring involving her child's father, Scooter Coggins, and Becky Seay's brother, Stephen. The latter was currently in Gwinnett County lock up on burglary charges.

All of this happened three months after the murder of nightclub owner Henry Jeffcoat, who was killed in a second planned attack to pilfer the two safes at his home. Safe-cracking cops, and their accomplices, were the number one target of all metro Atlanta police departments and a joint (Federal, State & Local) task force.

Moreover, there had been a string of safes cracked in and around Gwinnett County, including one owned by an attorney who reported $100,000.00 in cash and jewelry stolen. It was never recovered.

Burnette thanked Seay politely and told him to call if there was anything else. He was not interested in Seay's evidence, nor did he make any known effort to disrupt or question Amy Parker's Sugar Hill Gang or investigate the safe-cracking ring. The contradicting statements some gang members made to police in the robbery and murder of Emogene Thompson were accepted at face value with no corroboration required.

Burnette and GCPD were not concerned with or interested in any of these crimes.

When Sergeant Cline searched Chapel's patrol car and four lockers at the Northside Precinct, previously controlled by Chapel, he took into his possession Chapel's famous intel files. One can look back on the department's MDT transmissions to see numerous officers, investigators, detectives, and administrative brass often asking Chapel to check his files for intel on the latest hot pursuit.

Most of those files and micro tapes, including Chapel's intel and confidential informant files on the nefarious dealings of officer J. P. Morgan, Tookie, the Kautter chop shop surveillance, the safe robberies, the Coggins family, and many others, somehow disappeared. 'Lost' between Northside Precinct and Police Headquarters in Lawrenceville, 8.4 miles, according to Cline's 1995 testimony.

A GCPD internal review, known as the Powell Report, was done on the subject phone records: the victim's home and office, the firehouse, and Chapel's residence, precinct, and gym.

Lt. Powell also audited police logs, MDT traffic, and dispatch, as well as Chapel's financial records. After those records showed no unusual or suspicious activity, and no contact with the victim and therefore no meeting solicitation for the night of the murder the lynchpin of the prosecution's case, the District Attorney 'lost' the originals of the phone records and invoked an 'original records rule.' Porter asked the court to suppress the Powell Report from coming into evidence, and his motion was granted.

Following his suicide, a .38 caliber revolver was found on the nightstand in J. P. Morgan's master bedroom, noted by the medical examiner. The weapon was not subjected to standard police procedure. It was never tested nor viewed by Chapel's defense team, and its whereabouts are currently unknown.

A note, or perhaps confession typed by J. P. Morgan in the moments before he shot him-self in the head with his .40 caliber service weapon, was erased from his hard drives. According to Internal Affairs, the message and other evidence incriminating multiple parties, including at least one other officer, were irretrievably erased.

A secret deal made by the prosecution with the offending officer was hidden from the defense and the court. The offending officer, David Bodie Hurst, who did not testify in the Chapel case, or any other case on record, was allowed to keep $10,000.00 stolen from a GCPD evidence room because it was 'drug money anyway,' according to Danny Porter.

Hurst also had eight felony indictments reduced to one charge within two weeks of Chapel's guilty verdict. He was sentenced to community service.

The hidden prosecution of the victim's son, the State's star witness, for numerous fraud and criminal charges during the lead-up to the trial was also denied in open court by the District Attorney, now a matter of public record.

Reflecting on the long list of lost, hidden, manipulated, manufactured, or destroyed evidence in this case, one must begin to reflect on the preponderance of negligence, at the very least, and criminal framing and cover-up, at worst. How could this much evidentiary mishap or investigation failure occur in one case? Why would Gwinnett County do this to one of their own? Most importantly, how could Michael Chapel's trial go forward, in Gwinnett County, in this atmosphere of obvious obfuscation, incompetence, and malfeasance?

Once the industrial metro media, using GCPD and Danny Porter as virtually their only sources, got its manufactured outrage machine into high gear, the public's reasoned rage peaked, and a fair trial became impossible.

 **Fifteen**

With the greater Atlanta area enthralled with the Atlanta Braves' fifth straight pennant race and the feverish anticipation of the 1996 Summer Olympiad, the trial of the century was rolling on television screens around the country. Fledgling cable network, *Court TV*, was riding to the top of the ratings wave and needed a morning lead-in for the O. J. Simpson circus playing out in Los Angeles, CA.

The Atlanta press was treating the weeks leading to the Michael Chapel case as its own trial of the century. The *Atlanta Journal-Constitution* ran daily articles. There were nightly stories on all the local stations; and *CNN*, the Atlanta-based news giant, provided national coverage.

Court TV, also based in Atlanta, was allowed cameras in the courtroom and aired daily coverage of the trial. Dozens of reporters from every major news organization gave the Michael Chapel case the same attention as the Simpson trial, and America had a Trial-of-the-Century duo. *The State of Georgia V. Michael Harold Chapel* aired from 9 am to 1 pm Eastern Standard Time, and *The People V. O. J. Simpson* blew up television screens from 1 pm through the afternoon. Talking heads pontificated on both cases throughout the night.

NBC Dateline ran a favorable profile of District Attorney Danny Porter fashioning him as the diminutive truth seeker and defender of the courtroom. His fifteen minutes of fame well underway, Porter did not shy away from the cameras. He continually declared Chapel's guilt and implicated him in other crimes that GCPD and the District Attorney's office were 'looking into.'

None of those allegations ever led to evidence against Chapel. He was cleared of all suspicion, involving an armored car heist in Chamblee, Georgia, perpetrated by two men described as standing between 5' 8" and 5' 11", one Hispanic. A supplemental report by Chamblee Officer #165 noted several false leads provided by John Latty and his jailhouse snitch, Kenneth Brown.

Brown and Latty told Chamblee PD that Michael Chapel was expecting to have a love child with an African American gym member with whom they claimed Chapel was having an affair. She was said to be involved in covering Chapel's tracks.

Latty told Chamblee that Chapel had to get hearing aids because his eardrums were damaged by firing the .50 weapon inside the confines of the getaway van used in the Armored Car Robbery.

Chamblee actually did police work and noted that medical records proved that Chapel was prescribed the hearing aids long before the Armored Car Robbery. It was also impossible for Chapel to get a woman pregnant in 1993. He had a vasectomy in the late '80s.

Further, Chapel was cleared of all connections to the WBAC, the infamous band of murderous roid-raging cops in the Atlanta Metro, once the toxicology reports on Chapel's blood work returned negative.

All of his weapons were cleared as well, and virtually all of the members of the WBAC cooperated with authorities. None of them knew Michael Chapel.

GCPD Captain L. O. Cantrell's son, Kevin Cantrell, a convicted meth and crack dealer, sent a letter to the District Attorney clarifying a conversation the two had on the phone the previous Friday regarding a written statement Cantrell was to send to Porter. He said, *"I have no problem sending you a written statement against ex-officer Michael Chapel. My problem is this, I don't want to write a statement against Chapel and send it to you before I know what can be done for me."*

Fifteen

In addition to what the District Attorney could do for him, Cantrell asked to have his family put into a protection program. Eventually, the District Attorney would have Cantrell interviewed, and he implicated Chapel in a protection racket. His proof of this scheme was a twenty-five-dollar check, written to Iron Works Gym, the amount of the membership fee at Iron Works for one month.

The jailhouse snitches came out of the woodwork to implicate Chapel in return for curried favors from the GCPD and the DA. For Latty, and now Danny Porter steadfast in his trial strategy, the source of information was not important—only the number of people telling the same story the prosecution needed the public to hear.

Of course, that did not apply to the numerous persons, jailhouse snitches, and reputable citizens who came forward with reports of Michael Chapel having been set up. Those reports went ignored.

One such reputable citizen, Dana Blount, an accounting department employee at the Buford Auto Plaza, went to the home of a relative to retrieve her troubled niece, who was falling into drug abuse and running with Amy Parker's Sugar Hill Gang.

While waiting for her niece to pack, Blount observed Michael Thompson bragging about the money he intended to win in a proposed lawsuit. Blount heard Michael Thompson proclaim, "Michael Chapel didn't kill my mom, but I need him to be convicted of it so I can get millions from Gwinnett County." Blount and numerous named witnesses heard Michael Thompson make this proclamation. The information was brought forward to GCPD and the District Attorney. All ignored.

The truth of Michael Chapel's impeccable service record, his stellar reputation within the department, and a community was quickly forgotten and intentionally corrupted. In the Court of Public Opinion, he was branded an icy, arrogant cowboy boot-wearing dirty cop, out of control and out for blood to quench a desperate need for money. *Creative Loafing*, which carried a popular police blotter in its newspaper, called Chapel '*The Most Despicable Man in Georgia.*'

During opening statements at the August 1995 trial, Porter made much of Chapel's finances to show desperate straits before the murder and a sudden infusion immediately thereafter. Porter told the jury that Michael Chapel had asked a friend for a $1,500 loan in January that had not been paid back. He also disclosed that the family had received a notice from the IRS of a zero-base audit that could disallow up to $4,000 in expenses claimed on the Chapel's 1992 taxes. A truck had been voluntarily returned to the bank rather than be repossessed, a sign of desperate times.

Porter does not explain to the jury that most of Chapel's expenditures, including the rent and utilities on the Iron World Gym, were paid as they usually were, through the gym's business checking account, via check, and in the standard time frame, according to the landlord. She told investigators that Chapel was normally late by a week or two but always paid and was not considered problematic.

Porter does not explain that the returned truck, to avoid repossession, had occurred three years prior and had no bearing on the Chapel's finances in 1993. The IRS audit, which could have resulted in additional tax liability, could have also resulted in an overpayment and refund, as is often the case in routine, mail-in tax audits, such as the one faced by the Chapels. When audits result in additional taxes owed by the taxpayer, the IRS representatives negotiate an easy payback plan according to the taxpayer's ability to pay. In the overwhelming majority of cases, audits do not result in the wanton murder of an innocent grandmother.

Porter also failed to inform the jury that the Chapels ran a cash business. Many businesses in 1993, like Iron World Gym, remained as they had been since the founding of the country, cash and carry. Between the average $2,500 revenue from the gym, and approximately $1,000 from side gigs common among law enforcement officers, and $1,600 in tips from Eren's part-time waitressing job, the Chapels regularly brought in $5,100 a month in cash and approximately $3,500 per month from his GCPD paycheck. Thus, expenditures and deposits of $2,500 were not void of legitimacy, as Porter intimated. The multiple accounts Porter was referring to were the Chapels' family checking account and the Iron World Gym's business checking account. Neither were new, secret, or offshore accounts, which the Chapels did not have, yet patently Porter wished for the jury to see it that way.

It is reasonable to believe that an officer with an annual family income of $84,000, living in a modest starter home, without any gambling or drug habits, might ferret away $400 to spend on his one hobby – hunting.

The $600 cash spent on tee-shirts to sell at the gym was a recurring and customary purchase of goods to be sold at retail, ordered well before the murder took place. According to the loan-giver, Jack Dudley, the purchase was part of the reason for the small business loan.

There was no collection effort underway despite Porter's claims that this money was past due. The loan had also been withdrawn, in all $100 bills, from the same bank used by Dudley and both Emogene Thompson and the Chapels.

The internal financial audit, conducted by GCPD Lt. Powell stated, *"This may be crucial to the case since, from the business account, it appears Chapel had a financial problem in January and possibly February 1993, but had recovered from this problem prior to the homicide in April."*

Porter asked the judge to suppress Powell's report on the grounds that it relied on the phone records that Porter himself provided to Powell. Those records, the original copies subpoenaed from the appropriate entities, were 'lost' by Porter. Georgia's obscure and now obsolete 'Original Records' requirement for evidentiary proceedings was invoked. Porter knew that the Powell Report would be devastating to his case because it essentially exonerates Chapel, so he simply 'lost' his own records.

I'll let you decide if this was gross negligence or a more sinister malfeasance. The judge rewarded Porter for it, either way.

During Porter's opening statement, he describes the crime scene and the investigative efforts of the GCPD. He indicates that they 'sealed the scene and began to process it as you would expect the police to do with any crime scene, especially a brutal murder on the side of a busy highway. He also said, *"The first thing they did was contact her son."*

While one could argue that borrowing a couple of cones from the muffler shop and loosely placing yellow tape a few inches away from the car might have been considered sealing a crime scene in Andy Taylor's Mayberry, such actions are a far cry from sealing a crime scene in 1990's metro Atlanta. As a juror would later point out, there were 'many hands and bodies' in and around the crime scene during GCPD's investigation.

Michael Chapel

The security of the scene and the processing of the evidence comes further into question when one realizes that critical evidence, known in 1995 only to the prosecution and police investigators, was suppressed, destroyed, and manipulated. Evidence logs were altered or fabricated in the lead-up to the trial, and the defense was routinely denied access to critical exculpatory evidence.

It is also curious that Porter leads the jury to believe that the man who would soon be the State's star witness, Emogene Thompson's son, Michael Thompson, was contacted first by police in the ordinary course of what he is apparently trying to portray as a competent and routine investigation. In fact, Mr. Thompson arrived at the scene of the murder, unsolicited, just minutes after the police arrived on the scene. He was held at bay and unable to see the victim in the car, or if there even was a victim in the car, yet he acted distraught at the passing of his mother.

A responding fireman described the act, "He showed up right after we did, and was held away from the car, he had his hands over his face wailing, and when he removed his hands from his face, while I was looking right at him, there wasn't a tear in his eyes."

Nonetheless, Thompson questioned Detective Ervin at the scene, repeatedly, not about his mother's condition but the whereabouts of her purse.

Porter informed the jury that Chapel was secretly investigating the burglary at Emogene Thompson's home on Craig Drive. *"The key there is he never filed an incident report. He never logged it on his daily activity sheet that he had ever been in contact with Emogene Thompson. It wasn't until the body was discovered, and he was told of the fact that he came forward."*

Porter did not disclose to the jury that Michael Chapel's two contacts with the victim were initiated through police department communication channels from the victim herself, and therefore already on the record. When Chapel left the first call, where the victim refused to press charges against her son, he notified dispatch code thirty-two, no report requested.

Immediately after notifying dispatch of 'no report requested,' he briefed his supervisor, Sergeant D. E. Stone, while only two blocks from the victim's home. Chapel informed his superior officer on the call and began to fill out a report at his request. The investigators later found this report in his do bag, where Chapel indicated it would be located.

Porter also failed to disclose that Chapel reminded his superior officer of these contacts immediately upon learning of the murder. Following Stone's direction, Chapel notified the lead investigator and briefed him less than an hour later, providing in full detail his contacts with Emogene Thompson and subsequent investigation, all of which remain on record at the time of this writing.

Sixteen

*D*uring *Porter's opening argument,* he said, *"After his arrest, physical ev-idence was then gathered by the GCPD. The tire had already been removed from the vehicle. It had been determined that it was punctured by a single-edge sharp instrument, which is scientific talk for a knife."*

What Porter conveniently omits is the scientific term for no-evidence-ty-ing-Chapel-to-said-knife.

Curiously, he also forgot the scientific term for 'we found and confiscat-ed all of Chapel's knives, and they were all dual-edge blades, thus not the knife in question.'

He also neglects to share with the courtroom that the defense has a legal and constitutional right to examine the evidence, like the alleged sin-gle-edge punctures on the tire, which disappeared in police custody, as would a long line of evidence to follow. The prosecution failed to inform the jury how or when it was determined whether the tire had been run flat or if it went flat where it sat, as they claimed.

"A rain jacket which was recovered from a locker at the Northside Precinct, to which the defendant had sole access, was discovered to have high-velocity blood spatter of human origin. You will hear that the source or one of the only sources of high-velocity blood splatter is to be standing within 18 inches of someone when a bullet impacts their body."

Allowing Porter the benefit of the doubt because he may not have realized at that moment the lengths that he would go to in the coming years to deny efforts to test said rain jacket for DNA. He declined to inform the jury that the only testing ever done on the rain gear was GSR (gunshot residue) testing. The size 6-X yellow rain jacket, worn by Officer Chapel, was tested only for gunshot residue.

Notably, the rain gear worn by Officer Chapel as he allegedly shot Emogene Thompson twice in the head, at point-blank range with a .38 revolver, conclusively left zero gunshot residue.

It is also notable that the driver's door, partially opened window, overhead door jamb, and ceiling did not contain high-velocity blood spatter or any blood at all. The absence of blood spatter in these areas makes it hard to comprehend how a rubber rain jacket outside the vehicle in the pouring rain could be so contaminated.

"And finally," Porter said, *"the state recovered the seat of the defendant's patrol car. Right before being released back into service, and the defendant was already in custody, it was decided, based on a number of factors, to run one more test on the car, and the police here ran what is known as a luminol test. And when the luminol process was applied to the seat on the armrest and the edge of the passenger seat, it luminesced in the presence of blood."*

Oddly, Mr. Porter does not expound on the factors that led to that one last test right before the car was released back into service. It might be interesting to know what inspired Steve Cline's hunch that ID Techs (CSI) should run a luminol test specifically on the front seat—he directed them to test that area and not the rest of the car. Curiously, the vehicle had already been luminol tested and thoroughly searched, which produced negative results for blood.

The jury might have benefited from the knowledge that GCPD forgot to secure the vehicle in its gated and locked impound yard. Instead, the vehicle was left at GCPD headquarters in the large, unprotected, and unmonitored parking lot for a week. This provided zero chain of custody from when the vehicle was first processed by ID Techs (and cleared) up until the last test that magically produced a positive result.

At his conclusion of the opening, Mr. Porter put forward that Emogene

Sixteen

Thompson's blood-covered purse, containing the $7,000.00 Officer Chapel was so desperate to possess, was taken from her car seconds after the fatal shots were fired. In Officer Chapel's haste and arrogance, he tossed the purse into his patrol car, where it deposited 40 nanograms of the victim's blood on the top side of the deployed armrest in the defendant's patrol car.

Several issues arise from this conclusion. First, ID Tech Mary Ann White would later testify that she had deployed the armrest during the first search. It is noteworthy that the sides of the armrest and the top fabric retained the original dark blue color, unlike the bottom of the seat rest, and the driver's and passenger's seat all equally faded from exposure to sunlight. Due to his size, computer, and law enforcement equipment, Officer Chapel operated his shop (vehicle) with the armrest undeployed in its fully upright position.

It was virtually impossible for the bloody purse to have deposited the blood where it was found in Chapel's vehicle. It is equally hard to believe that Officer Chapel decided to utilize his armrest this one time following the murder of a defenseless grandmother in cold blood on the side of a busy highway wearing a Big Bird costume while standing in front of his department-identified patrol car with blue lights flashing.

Mr. Porters' conclusion in this case, that the bloody purse deposited the blood, in a nearly impossible manner, onto the top of Officer Chapel's seat rest, before Officer Chapel drove away, pocketed the money, and then disposed of the purse became impossible shortly after the trial when Emogene's missing purse was suddenly located.

The purse was found by a young neighbor playing near the back of Emogene Thompson's trailer in an area that had been grid searched by GCPD multiple times before and after Officer Chapel's arrest, making it impossible for inmate Chapel to have deposited the purse in its final hiding place.

It becomes impossible to believe that the bloody purse deposited the forty nanograms of blood on the top of Chapel's upright armrest when one learns that extensive testing on the purse's exterior and interior, including all its contents, showed that no blood was present, and no blood traces could be found.

Michael Chapel

The purse was not in Emogene Thompson's vehicle when the shots were fired. It did not deposit forty nanograms of blood to an improbable part of Officer Chapel's patrol car. It was not deposited under a piece of plywood near her trailer by Michael Harold Chapel.

Next, one must consider the DNA evidence tested by the Georgia Bureau of Investigation's (GBI) crime lab on behalf of GCPD.

The swath of cloth from Chapel's patrol car was cut from the seat and run through forensic DNA testing, a process Mr. Porter referred to as a five-probe test. Each probe, or genetic yardstick, is put against the subject material and compared to the known material to see if the probes or yardsticks line up.

Through testimony, we learn in order to read the yardstick, a center of the subject and known material must be ascertained. Instead of using the high-tech DNA testing equipment designed for this purpose, the centers were '*eye-balled.*' When the desired results were not obtained, the manually adjusted center was modified. You will also learn that this type of testing is no longer considered viable scientifically. Dr. Choi, a scientist, and DNA expert, concluded that the testing done in this case was unreliable, at best.

Porter concluded his opening statement. *"The verdict that speaks the truth, in this case, is that Michael Thompson...or excuse me, Michael Chapel is guilty of malice murder."* Whether a Freudian slip or the verdict that points to the truth, one is quickly reminded of the statement Porter made a year and a half after this trial and conviction, printed on the front page of the *Gwinnett Daily Post* on January 1, 1997, *"I would also like to find out who it is that really killed Emogene Thompson."*

Seventeen

"*Congratulations, Johnny!*" Danny Porter approached Johnny Moore and the defense team on the final day of testimony to concede defeat. "It looks like you're going to get Mike off. Maybe I should offer a plea deal?"

Moore, who had been feeling good about Chapel's chances for acquittal, mainly because of the circumstantial nature of the confusing case Porter had presented, accepted the congratulatory comments at face value. With a slightly inflated sense of confidence, he responded, "Well, thanks, Danny. You have been a worthy adversary, but we feel good about Mike's chances. No plea deal."

"That's understandable," Porter said, trying to sound defeated. "At this point, I just want to get out of here without too much more embarrassment."

"You've got nothing to be embarrassed about, counselor," Johnny said, his self-importance rising with each syllable.

"I don't know about that, Moore," Porter said. "PD's case hasn't done me any favors. I figure by the time you carve me up in summation. I might as well drop out of the upcoming election for District Attorney. No way I get reelected."

"I wouldn't worry about one case, Danny. You've done a good job for the citizens. They won't hold this case against you." Moore said, sounding like a guidance counselor. "I'm just hoping you take it easy on me."

"Why don't we take it easy on each other, John?" Porter sank the hook. "I'll let you make your summation without interruption, no objections, you just make your case, and I'll make mine, we'll let the chips fall where they may?"

Amazingly, this deal was made. Judge Bishop expressed concern to the defense. His concern was noted but ignored, and the arrangement went forward. Johnny Moore gave Danny Porter the final word and surrendered his ability to challenge any falsehoods or procedural errors presented to the jury by the prosecution's final words.

Johnny Moore had managed to snatch defeat from the jaws of victory in a stunning negotiation that allowed Danny Porter to spin a summation story not grounded in facts, evidence, or logic. His summation went well beyond the evidence presented, which flies in the face of codified jurisprudence.

The last words the jury heard were the false narrative that Danny Porter fed to the Atlanta press and the nation since late April 1993. It was sensational, convenient, and utterly devoid of any factual evidence.

"A hundred witnesses, three hundred exhibits later, our job is almost done, and your job will continue as you begin to deliberate what is the truth of this case." Porter began.

One hundred witnesses testified in the case of the State of Georgia vs. Michael Harold Chapel. Three hundred exhibits were used, and to say that the case presented to the jury was primarily circumstantial and well within the realm of reasonable doubt is truly an understatement. A detailed discussion of the jury will follow, but first, one needs to examine the story spun by District Attorney Danny Porter entirely.

"The defendant has raised a defense, and the Court will charge you of what's called alibi. Alibi is a legal defense that says it was impossible for me to be at the scene of the crime; I could not be there; I was somewhere else. And the defendant has presented witnesses to that. You should consider the testimony regarding alibi, you should consider the credibility of that testimony, and you should con-

sider the quality of that testimony just like any other witness."

"And you should also look at one basic fact. It's that the defendant's evidence is subject to the same scrutiny that the states is. Once the defendant takes up the burden to bring you evidence, he's subject to the same scrutiny as the state."

"And that brings us to the idea of credibility of witnesses or believability of witnesses."

To spin his tale, Porter must first convince the jury that Chapel was not somewhere else, and to do that, Porter needs you to question the testimony of six dedicated and credible first responders. The C Shift from Firehouse Fourteen virtually all placed Chapel at the firehouse adjacent to the police precinct from 2030 until 2200. To get you to question these men, Porter presents two other first responders, Chapel's 'friends' Officer Brian Reddy and Sergeant D. E. Stone.

Reddy lied. Reddy admitted to lying the night of Chapel's interrogation, while Latty and Burnette were yet accusing Chapel of lying due to the discrepancy in Chapel's statement and the statement of Reddy.

"Why would your friend Brian Reddy lie?"

Chapel was asked repeatedly as if Chapel was casting aspersions on his honorable friend *'who would take a bullet for you.'* Chapel's response, *"I don't know why he's saying that. Maybe he is mistaken, maybe he is mixing his dates because that's where I was, that's who I was with, and that's what we did."*

"How could Brian forget it? Brian's no dummy. Brian's very astute, bright man and very experienced in police work. He knows the importance of things; he knows the importance. He knows the importance."

After hours of this badgering, Latty walked into the interrogation room and said, *"Well, Mike, Reddy was mistaken, you was at the firehouse like you said, but now he says you left. So, you was there, but you left around 2130."*

So here we have Brian Reddy, who is very astute, very experienced in police work, who knows the importance of things, hours into the interrogation of Chapel, and hours into his statement, changing his story. Even if we accept the new story as the accurate story, the timeline still does not work. Witnesses saw the police officer, who Latty and District Attorney Danny Porter would describe as laying-in-wait, as early as 2045 and almost continuously until after 2130.

On the night of Chapel's arrest, D. E. Stone would support Chapel's timeline of events stating that Chapel was with him and Reddy at the firehouse until approximately 2200. He recollected the timing because he said that he left about twenty minutes after Chapel to phone his wife. Phone records indicate that he phoned his wife at 2217, exactly twenty-one minutes after the dispatch transmission to Chapel.

Yet Porter was able to get Stone to remember differently for trial, and he agreed with Reddy's second version events that Chapel left around 2130.

Reddy and Stone also admitted to falsifying their log sheets on the night in question. Reddy's log sheet places him less than a mile from the murder scene within the window of the crime.

So, why would they lie? The burden to answer that question lies with the state, even as Porter lied to the jury and shifted the burden without fear of objection. What we do know, however, is that they did lie.

"Now, when you take the law that I've just described to you, and you take the facts, the conclusion which speaks the truth, in this case, is that Mike Chapel came into contact for the first time with Emogene Thompson on April 3rd, 1993, when he reported... when he responded to the report of a theft of her money, that he decided at that time that she was a doper. He decided at that time that he needed the money, and so he stayed in contact with her." Porter continues.

"And on the night of April the 15th, he lured her to the Gwinnco Muffler on the pretense of continuing to work her case. He was running the boo. And he got her out there at about nine-thirty or nine-forty that night, and with two shots, he ended her life. He stole her money, and in the process of taking the money out of her purse, he transferred her blood to the seat of his patrol car, and then he left. And he left and had the misfortune of driving by Karl Kautter. He went on — he got a call. He went on to the call, but he left, saying he had problems of his own. And he did."

To believe the state's theory in this case, we must assume that Chapel plotted his scheme to murder Ms. Thompson in her living room on that first call on April 3rd, 1993. He must have also prearranged a meeting for the night of April 15, 1993, some twelve days in advance to compare the serial numbers of bills that he intended to find at some point in the intervening days. Now, he could have prearranged that meeting during the follow-up call, but the only follow-up call took place on April 4, 1993, so we are still talking about an eleven-day window.

Interestingly, there is evidence that someone was thinking about the imminent crime on April 4, 1993. An associate of Amy Parker, Barry Graham, snapped a Polaroid of Chapel's police car, sitting in front of Emogene Thompson's trailer, and sent it to GCPD several weeks later as evidence that Chapel was stalking the victim.

Even though Emogene Thompson initiated the follow-up call through the police department, same as the first call on April 3, it would have been informative to learn from Mr. Graham exactly why he took this photo and what he intended to prove with it.

Unfortunately, Mr. Graham could not testify as scheduled because he allegedly killed himself with a shotgun blast that no one heard. GCPD SWAT surrounded Mr. Graham at his Lilburn home after GCPD was called to an alleged hostage situation. The alleged hostage walked safely out the front door unmolested, leaving Graham alone and alive inside the dwelling. Shortly after that, twenty-five SWAT officers converged on the residence and set off a flashbang grenade upon entry.

Sergeant Steve Cline, the ranking officer on the scene, would report that Graham was apparently dead from a shotgun blast before GCPD's breach, despite no one on the SWAT team or any witnesses having heard the shotgun go off.

Eighteen

"*It has never been my habit to comment upon the case put up by a defendant in my argument to the jury. It has never been my habit to comment upon the evidence the defendant puts up in his own defense. But in this case, after listening to the evidence and listening to the argument of counsel and the pack of misdirection, innuendo, and outright falsehoods that have been presented to this jury, I feel that I must.*" Porter said.

"*This defendant has engaged in a pattern of misdirection and misinterpretation from the outset of this case that has been conducted through his attorneys and through his own testimony on a variety of fronts.*"

This is classic projection. The state presented numerous witnesses that changed their story to fit Porter's narrative, misrepresented other testimony, relied on demonstrably false testimony, cast aspersions on the firemen, unbiased citizens, and respected experts. The state intentionally withheld exculpatory evidence and purposely suppressed the results of its investigative efforts when those efforts exonerated Chapel.

Porter continued, "*Let's look at the first defense he wants you to put up, or he wants you to believe. He has dragged every police officer in Gwinnett County by innuendo into this courtroom. He has dragged every upstanding, fine officer that all of us know in an effort to divert your attention from the overwhelming evidence of his guilt.*"

"*He's gone so far as to specifically name people as suspects, and the state has had to waste your time and my time shooting those suspects out of the saddle one by one. The first person they brought in was the Sugar Hill city marshal. The Sugar Hill city marshal didn't kill Emogene Thompson. The shooting occurred and was done by a right-handed shooter. Chris Robertson is left-handed."*

Porter wants the jury to be angry at Michael Chapel for asking the same questions GCPD and his investigators were asking before John Latty held a roadside tribunal on the side of Highway 20 and decided that Chapel was the bad guy. Nonetheless, according to none other than John Latty, Chris Robertson was a suspect, Latty said they were looking at the Sugar Hill marshal, but he was a southpaw.

The fact that there was no actual proof presented that Robertson is a 'southpaw' notwithstanding, his alibi for the time of the murder is unknown. He fit the description of the cop on the scene much better than Chapel. And he lied to GCPD regarding his contacts with Amy Parker and the Sugar Hill Gang.

A credible forensic report illustrates several issues with the conclusion that the shots were fired by a right-handed shooter. The forensic evidence in this case that experts have examined suggests that Emogene Thompson was shot from the back seat by a left-handed shooter. The physical evidence eliminates the State's theory of the crime.

Porter continued and said that Chapel, *"dragged every upstanding, fine police officer in Gwinnett County by innuendo into this courtroom."*

While that is demonstrably false, it does beg the question, how many upstanding fine police officers did GCPD drag by innuendo into the secret Northside investigation? Certain officers were demoted, transferred, or otherwise disciplined by the department in connection with that investigation.

Danny Porter and the media chided Chapel as a wild conspiracy theorist, shot-gunning accusations against these fine upstanding officers. Chapel claimed to be investigating some of them before what he characterized as a set-up to neutralize his investigations.

Is it that far-fetched when you consider sixty-one officers were transferred or disciplined for infractions such as theft of property and cash

Eighteen

from the evidence room? A Captain was demoted for concealing intel about several burglaries in the community. Another officer was caught destroying evidence. There was a litany of other charges that the public has been denied it is right to know about, as that investigation report has remained illegally sealed since 1994.

The fact is, Michael Chapel was famous within the department for his intel gathering and made it known to certain officials, whom he trusted, that his intel-gathering uncovered information regarding the nefarious dealings of multiple officers.

The related intel files were confiscated from Chapel's lockers at the precinct, from the trunk of his patrol car, and from his office at Iron Works gym after his arrest. Detective Steve Cline collected them and, according to Cline's testimony, lost them during the 8.4 mile drive from the precinct to GCPD Headquarters.

The cover-up was not limited to Cline. Bodie Hurst went into J. P. Morgan's home office immediately following Morgan's suicide and destroyed what John Latty expected was a suicide note. Some have speculated to include a final confession. Hurst destroyed two hard drives that contained criminal evidence against Morgan, Hurst, and at least one other individual, GCPD later admitted.

More importantly, we must consider who was present when Bodie Hurst destroyed all this evidence. We learn from the Medical Examiner's report that GCPD Chief Wayne Bolden, Assistant Chief Carl White, Lt. Charlie Bishop, Sergeant R. C. Davis, and Investigator B. J. Tkacik were all present on the scene when Bodie Hurst committed multiple felonies to cover up an unknown number of other crimes.

It is irrefutable that there were several dirty cops within the rank and file of GCPD. When Danny Porter negotiated a secret deal with Bodie Hurst that allowed Hurst to keep $10,000 of ill-gotten gain and avoid jail time for eight felonies in trade to keep his mouth shut, Porter removed any doubt that he too was actively engaged in the cover-up.

In summation, Porter continued. *"And when that didn't work, the next one he brought in was Brian Reddy, his friend. He's willing to sacrifice his friend in his desperation to evade the consequences of his act. But Brian Reddy didn't kill Emogene Thompson. If we're certain that anyone was at that fire station all night on April the 15th, it was Brian Reddy because Reddy is clearly alibied by the firefighters. They remember him. Reddy is alibied by Chapel's good friend Don Stone. He remembers. And the firearm that Reddy owns has been absolutely excluded by Kelly Fite as the murder weapon."*

With a friend like Brian Reddy, you have to wonder why Chapel needed any enemies. Reddy demonstrably and admittedly lied about Chapel's whereabouts. He did not mix the dates. He was not mistaken; Reddy lied. He only altered his lie to a slightly more plausible lie when D. E. Stone swore to the truth of the matter, that Chapel was with Stone and Reddy at the firehouse, with the six firemen.

Porter also tells the jury that the firearm owned by Reddy, a Charter Arms .38 that fit the subject weapon, was absolutely excluded by Kelly Fite as the murder weapon. He fails to remind the jury that Reddy 'forgot' he had that gun until right before the trial when Porter gave him heads-up that his favored gun shop was about to be subpoenaed.

Porter also neglected to remind the jury that Kelly Fite admitted that he could not determine if the gun tested had its original barrel or if a replacement barrel was affixed to the gun before testing.

Finally, Porter says, *"If we're confident of anything, it's Brian Reddy's whereabouts."* There is only one tiny problem with that, Reddy's police log sheet, written by himself, places him within a mile of the crime scene during the window of death. But that's okay. Reddy explained – *he lied.*

He lied on his log sheet, he lied in his interview, and he lied about his gun. It seems the only thing we can be sure of with Brian Reddy – he lies.

"So, who's next? Who do we look for next? J. P. Morgan. J. P. Morgan killed himself about fifteen days after the murder of Emogene Thompson. It was actually about twenty-two days. And in the most shameful – in the most shameful attempt to evade responsibility, Michael Chapel is prepared to malign the reputation of a dead man, a man who can't come in like Brian Reddy did and defend himself. He's prepared to climb on the shoulders of a dead man to escape his responsibility."

Eighteen

Judge Bishop would not allow the defense to delve into the suicide of J. P. Morgan or the subsequent destruction and cover-up of the evidence of his wrongdoing. This was critical to Chapel's defense from the outset. Chapel maintains that his investigation of dirty cops, specifically including Morgan and Hurst, made him the target of the set-up, and he was now on trial as a result.

Nonetheless, Bishop muted the defense on the issue. Yet here we have Porter, without fear of objection, using Morgan's death as a bludgeon against Chapel.

What is also quite telling, as to the 'Honorable' Daniel J. Porter's integrity, is that Porter knew something at that moment unknown to the judge, the jury, the defense, or anyone outside of the Chapel prosecution team. Porter was negotiating with Bodie Hurst, who was under felony indictment for eight charges, and he was secretly prosecuting his star witness, Michael Thompson, for multiple fraud charges.

Porter had been moved by court order to disclose all deals with any witnesses or connected persons. Porter told the judge in open court that no such deals were in place nor would be made without prior disclosure. We now know that Porter lied to the court and was, in fact, actively concealing the prosecution of Thompson and working out 'sweetheart' deals for both Thompson and Hurst.

It is also noteworthy that J. P. Morgan's whereabouts on the night of the murder are unknown to the defense, despite Porter informing the jury that his whereabouts had been determined. Determined how? By whom? Where is that report?

Morgan fit the description of the cop on the scene, he had access to the department's spare patrol car, and he killed himself as soon as the defense team began naming him as the mastermind of the set-up of Chapel and threatened to expose his illegal deeds.

Porter notes that Morgan's weapon was cleared, which is true of his .40 caliber service weapon. Still, there is no record of what happened to the .38 caliber revolver the Medical Examiner observed lying on his nightstand; another weapon matching the subject weapon that disappeared in the custody of GCPD.

Porter also said, *"And beginning with statements that were made in the Hall County jail that began the investigation to clear J. P. Morgan, J. P. Morgan was cleared."*

Cleared because Porter says so? How was he cleared? None of the evidence of that investigation was provided. An Open Record's Act request procured only the aforementioned Medical Examiner's Report that revealed the existence of the .38 previously unknown to the defense.

Porter also claims tests were run on Morgan's car that he says, *"Ironically was the same kind of car driven by Michael Chapel."*

It is hard to understand why it was ironic, as virtually the whole department drove a car like Chapel's. It is also not important that Morgan's assigned patrol car was cleared because the patrol car witnessed at the scene was not Morgan's assigned car or the car that Chapel was indelibly linked to on the night in question.

The car witnessed at the scene could have only been the precinct's spare car that Morgan could access like other precinct members. Oddly Enough, that car, the precinct's spare, was never tested for the record, and like so much crucial evidence, in this case, it disappeared in GCPD custody. It simply vanished.

The true irony is that there is significantly more evidence that identifies Morgan at the scene than there ever was of Chapel. According to District Attorney Porter the investigation into Morgan began, *"with the statements that were made in the Hall County jail."* Morgan learned that he was being investigated and decided to take the coward's way out while Michael Chapel continues to proclaim his innocence.

Nineteen

Porter went on. "And then, finally, worst of all, every police officer who walked into this courtroom, from Rick Winderweedle, who did nothing more than pass on a message, to an officer who's been introduced by innuendo, as Defendant's 38, has been indirectly accused of the murder of Emogene Thompson and had to defend themselves."

It is unclear what Porter was ranting about, but the insinuation that anyone accused Sergeant Winderweedle of murder is delusional at best and prejudicial slander in reality.

Winderweedle's testimony, however, destroys one of the state's foundational arguments in this case. The state argued that Chapel formulated his plan to rob and murder Emogene Thompson on April 3, 1993, and from that point forward, he began to stalk her to set his murderous plot in motion. According to the state, Chapel's April 4 visit was the first act in furtherance of that scheme.

We learn from his testimony that Winderweedle received a phone call at the precinct from a woman identifying herself as Emogene Thompson on April 4th. This caller requested that Officer Chapel contact her, a message that Winderweedle then passed on to Chapel. Both established contacts that Chapel had with the victim were initiated by the victim and communicated through the department to Chapel, and therefore, not part of any 'stalking' scheme.

"Even Rudowski, who didn't even work in the northside precinct – he worked in the Westside Precinct, which is down at Jimmy Carter Boulevard – the defendant has the audacity to accuse him, because he wants to divert – he wants to divert your attention. He wants you to do anything but pay attention to the evidence."

Again, it is unclear who wants to divert attention. Still, since no one, aside from Porter, accused Rudowski of anything, it is apparent that Porter wanted the jury to pay attention to anything but the evidence.

"Well, then, the accusation against other officers, that doesn't work. So, the next step is, let's put up an alibi. Let's put up the firefighters. They'll remember."

They did remember, just as the statements they wrote, signed, and turned into Captain Hunnicutt shortly after Chapel's arrest, that Chapel was at the firehouse. One fireman did not give a specific time of departure in 1993 or 1995. When prompted by the District Attorney, one fireman remembered a movie playing on a premium channel that none of the other firemen or the three police officers remembered. This could have been the entertainment that evening, proposed the prosecutor, and the firefighter agreed. Because this movie ended at 2130, it allowed Porter to imply that Chapel left the firehouse between 2130 and 2140.

If true, it allowed Chapel to arrive at the scene of the murder at about the time that Emogene Thompson arrived, allowed him a total of roughly three minutes to perpetrate the crime, be seen by nearly a half dozen witnesses before 'speeding off at 2156' according to John Latty.

This timeline, however, does not explain the police officer witnessed by a dozen people at the scene prior to 2140. Both Danny Porter at trial and John Latty, while interrogating Chapel, alleged that Chapel laid-in-wait for Emogene Thompson at the Muffler Shop from 2045 until 2145, leaving at 2156. This theory and the state's entire timeline are destroyed by the testimony of the firemen, even if you accept the altered and earlier departure time allowed by one of them.

It should not have been refutable that Chapel responded to dispatch at 2156 on the chronologically recorded police dispatch radio. If, as Chapel has maintained for twenty-eight years, he was standing fourteen inches away from the firehouse's chronologically recorded dispatch speaker, the tapes for this period would have cleared up any confusion whether Chapel was at the firehouse until approximately 2200. These tapes corroborated Chapel's alibi and the statements of five of the firemen. Unfortunately, according to John Latty, GCPD 'lost' the tapes after listening to them one time.

"So, the defendant then has to take another tack. He has to raise the issue of contamination, sloppy police work."

"Ladies and gentlemen, I'm going to ask you to look at one defense exhibit as evidence of sloppy police work. In this box, there's a piece – there's a pack of Carefree Sugarless Gum, and there's a package of soup that was held by the Gwinnett County police department for almost two years in case that it had any evidentiary value and was finally released to the defendant. Would a police department that kept a pack of gum as potential evidence be sloppy? Is that not meticulous police work? Is that not indicative of meticulous police work?"

For the love of Lady Justice! GCPD managed not to lose two items with no evidentiary value; therefore, GCPD is meticulous and competent!

Forget the fact that they secured the crime scene in such a loose and sloppy manner that evidence of the slashed tire was concealed from the CSI team by their own crime scene tape. Forget the fact that the suspect's vehicle, an alleged location of crucial evidence, was forgetfully (or perhaps intentionally) left outside the chain of custody, unsecured for a week. Forget that the yellow rose was removed from the crime scene (the victim's car) by GCPD and lost (or destroyed).

Forget the lost dispatch tapes. Forget that GCPD lost or 'discarded' a set of fingerprints from the dashboard of the victim's car. Forget that GCPD lost, destroyed, or otherwise failed to follow protocol for at least five .38 caliber weapons connected to this case.

Forget that GCPD lost track of two police cars, failed to search the vehicle driven by the victim's son that uniquely matched the description of a vehicle witnessed at the crime scene during the window of death, and released the crime scene (Emogene Thompson's car) to her son, Michael Thompson. According to none other than Danny Porter, Michael Thompson was the prime suspect in the initial theft that ignited this saga. *"The events of April of 1993 show clearly that Emogene Thompson had fourteen thou-*

sand dollars that she hid away for whatever reason and that half of it was stolen from her, probably by her son."

Michael Thompson was also GCPD's initial suspect in the murder. Porter wants the jury to forget that he made contradictory statements regarding his yet uncorroborated alibi and lied about contact with his drug dealer within an hour of Emogene Thompson's murder. Thompson had a motive beyond anyone connected to this case. Aside from the seven thousand dollars, Emogene Thompson was alleged to have had on her person when she died, Michael Thompson was the sole beneficiary of a $115,000.00 life insurance policy.

Finally, the .38 caliber weapon found at the American Inn, with two spent chambers, intentionally destroyed by GCPD, was located approximately fifty feet from the room Michael Thompson had stayed in four days prior. If any suspect, in this case, had motive, means, and opportunity, it was the victim's son, Michael Thompson.

Considering all the evidence lost, mishandled, unresolved, or uncorroborated, a mountain of evidence pointing to the involvement of other people, and that GCPD investigated in breach of its certification as a police department, it is hard to imagine describing the investigation of Michael Harold Chapel as anything but corrupt and sloppy. Criminally. Irreparably. Unconscionably sloppy.

"So, they have to come up with contamination. The blood on the seat came from somewhere else. Well, let's look at the sources of that contamination. Where is Emogene Thompson's blood going to come from if, in fact, it was planted on the seat."

Great question, Mr. Porter. This should be examined.

"Well, the first source is Emogene Thompson. They had to get some blood from Emogene Thompson, but they couldn't do that. Hal Bennett testified that he was with the body the whole time, that no one touched the body except the doctor, that no blood was drawn except what was put in the vials and delivered to the crime lab, and that he remained with the body until it was delivered to the funeral home. So, the body is out as the first source."

Who was with the body from 2200 on April 15 until 0800 on April 16 when the Sugar Hill Marshal was alone with the body? We know that a six-foot, 180 lb. white male was at the scene, alone with the body for some period of time during or shortly after the window of death. We also know that three or four individuals were with the body around 2200. Another vehicle appeared around midnight of the 15th. Presumably, that person was alone with the body, and from Jack Burnette's handwritten notes, we know that the Gwinnett County Sheriff disclosed to Danny Porter that *"someone else"* was seen at the muffler shop on the night in question.

Simple arithmetic derives at six or seven people who had access to the bleeding dead body unsecured and unmonitored for the better part of ten hours. At least two of those individuals had access to crime scene kits that allowed them to swab the blood and hermetically seal it until it could be unsealed and swabbed unto the armrest of a subject patrol car that sat unmonitored and unsecured for the better part of a week, or for any other use.

"But where was that trash can in relation to Unit 197 when the alleged mysterious person took the blood sample? That car was in the possession of Mike Chapel because the blood – and remember that the autopsy was conducted on April the 16th of 1993. It wasn't until a week later that Mike Chapel was arrested. It wasn't until five days after that the car was luminoled."

Oddly, Porter does not remind the jury of the first luminol test on April 23, when Chapel was arrested. That luminol test was conducted when the car transferred from Chapel's custody to the GCPD CSI team. Porter's argument would have merit if Emogene Thompson's blood was found on the armrest or the front seat – since the armrest was undeployed and upright according to ID Tech M.A. White, who testified that she lowered the armrest and left it down. However, the first search was negative. No blood. No incriminating evidence.

"So, in order to accept the contamination theory, you must believe that someone, some mysterious someone, went into the trash can, because we've ruled out the body, obtained a blood sample, held that blood sample in a liquid state for almost a week in anticipation of gaining control of Mike Chapel's car, and then they went in, and they put one tiny little smear on the armrest."

This case is so far past the Rubicon on a police department frame and cover-up that these alleged conspiracies scoffed at by Porter are not even hard to believe. The previously unknown presence of the GCPD hierarchy at the suicide and evidence destruction party at J. P. Morgan's house intimates that the dirty cops in Gwinnett County had made their way all the way to the top.

Consider the direct evidence that Jack Burnette manufactured a log sheet to conceal exculpatory evidence. He conspired with the aforementioned GCPD hierarchy to manufacture witnesses, according to his meeting notes. He blatantly lied to other Gwinnett County employees as to the veracity of the evidence against Chapel.

When one considers these facts, it is well within the realm of possibility that Burnette or one of the other investigators in this cabal obtained blood from one of the vials, the body, or blood-soaked trash cans. When one looks at the facts of this case, it becomes impossible to rule out blatant, intentional, and highly illegal wrongdoing on the part of the . Gwinnett County Police Department.

# Twenty

*A*n old lawyers' meme, 'if you can't dazzle them with brilliance then baffle them with bullshit,' seems to be the Porter summation strategy.

"So, the contamination system – contamination argument starts to disappear, so they have to come up with another one, another source for the blood. Somebody else gave us the blood. That's how the blood got on the car seat. Well, by his own test and by his own experts, we know that Mike Chapel didn't. That's not Mike Chapel's blood on that patrol car seat. Even his own experts acknowledge that. So, who else's blood is it? All the stories about putting a hand through the window of a car to apprehend an armed suspect don't help you anymore. Whose blood is it? And they come up with Ms. Cronic."

The esteemed District Attorney appears to be babbling here. There was no evidence presented that the blood in the patrol car was Chapel's blood or derived from the apprehension of an armed suspect. Porter is either lost or trying to baffle the jury by conjoining the armrest and rain-coat blood issues into a mass of confusion.

Even though the testing that identified Emogene Thompson's blood was 'unreliable at best' according to expert testimony, the blood on the armrest was almost certainly Emogene Thompson's blood. The source of that blood and the vehicle of its transfer is very much at issue.

Forensics concluded that the blood on the armrest was not a naturally occurring droplet. The blood was likely swabbed onto the armrest. Considering the questionable nature of the blood droplet and the lack of chain of custody of the patrol car, this blood contamination should never have been allowed into evidence.

"Ms. Cronic, who was probably the most credible witness in the entire defense case, who didn't even remember the police coming, who drove off a four-foot wall at the Buford post office and hit her head and bled. And there's one thing I want you to look at when you consider Ms. Cronic's case and the evidence that was put in. They have to use Ms. Cronic for one of two things. She either explains the blood in the patrol car, or she explains the blood on the raincoat, and they've chosen to go with the raincoat. When you look at the pictures that the defendant put in, he's not wearing a raincoat in those pictures. He's standing there with her car after it's driven off the wall in his sunglasses, and he's not wearing a raincoat. So Ms. Chronic absolutely cannot be the source of the blood either on his car or his raincoat."

Ah, the raincoat. The size 6-X police identified yellow raincoat that Porter had hanging from a hat stand in front of the jury like a high-velocity blood-spattered scarlet letter. It matters not if the less than half-dozen micro-dots of potentially human blood on Chapel's raincoat came from Ms. Cronic, the armed suspect, a dying horse, deer strikes, any of the hundreds of accidents or altercations Chapel worked in the 8.5 years since joining the GCPD. None of those things can be ruled out as the source because Danny Porter elected not to have the raincoat DNA or blood type tested.

Porter's reasoning for not testing the coat? $900. The prosecution of Officer Chapel cost the taxpayers of Gwinnett County nearly $500,000.00, yet Porter was so concerned with saving $900, the cost of the testing, that he refused to test the raincoat. He objected when Elizabeth Rogan pointed this out to the jury in summation, but the judge overruled.

The bottom line is Porter wanted the jury to believe that Chapel's raincoat was covered in Emogene Thompson's blood, but he was unwilling to have it tested to prove it. On the other hand, Chapel filed numerous motions over the last twenty-eight years asking for testing of the raincoat, only to have Porter oppose at every turn.

"Then we got Lieutenant Powell up, and the defendant attempted, through a

lengthy direct examination, to go into the MDT traffic, the telephone traffic, and the financial records. And it wasn't until my cross-examination that you realized that the data that Lieutenant Powell based his conclusions on was false from the very beginning. It was flawed. And I saw some of you throw your pens down, and I thought this is typical of the defendant's strategy in this case."

By false and flawed, Porter means that he got it excluded on a technicality. The technicality was that he, Porter himself, 'lost' the original records.

When Powell oversaw the Internal Affairs Investigation into Chapel linked to the WBAC joint task force and began to examine all the communication channels open to Chapel and the victim, Porter was alarmed to learn that there were precisely no unaccounted for or suspicious communications between Chapel and the victim. Porter became desperate when the 'Powell Report' went on to declare that Chapel's finances after the murder appeared the same as they had before the murder and from the inception of his accounts.

Powell, who was no friend to Chapel, used Xerox photocopies of the very records obtained and supplied by the district attorney's office to produce his report. Porter simply could not have the jury review the Powell Report. It was an analytical presentation of the facts that essentially destroys the entire case brought by the state and exonerates Chapel. To that end, Porter simply lost his original records and motioned the judge to exclude the report based on an obscure and now obsolete 'original records' rule in Georgia.

Typical of the prosecution (and the GCPD) in this case.

"It's typical that they didn't confront Mr. Kautter with his statement, 'I'll have to say.' They confronted Sergeant Cline. They didn't confront Ms. Burel about the telephone calls from Emogene Thompson. They confronted Lieutenant Powell. They didn't confront the witness who could tell you the truth. They confronted a commentator. And Lieutenant Powell is the perfect example of that."

Porter appears to believe it inappropriate to question the police investigators for any reason. Earlier, he likened cross-examination or the defense simply calling a witness to Michael Chapel accusing that witness of murdering Emogene Thompson. Remember he told the jury, *"Every police officer who walked into this courtroom, from Rick Winderweedle, who did nothing more than pass on a message, to an officer who's been introduced by innuendo, as Defendant's 38, has been indirectly accused of the murder of Emogene Thompson and had to defend themselves."*

Elizabeth Rogan might have been afraid she would be brought up on charges if she went so far as to ask Mrs. Burel why she lied about her phone conversations with Emogene Thompson, especially on the night in question. But Rogan did not need to take that risk. She could simply ask the professional policeman who examined the phone records. Did Mrs. Burel speak to Emogene Thompson continuously on the phone until 8:30 pm on the 15th, making at least six to eight separate phone calls as she had claimed?

"No."

So, we know Burel lied. Like Brian Reddy. We don't know why she lied, but we know that she lied.

Porter begins to wrap up his closing fables with cries afoul that Chapel's demeanor was too calm. He smiled at his wife; a guy is so arrogant that he wore cowboy boots to trial, and then he goes in for the kill, pun intended.

"And then finally he brings the final insult. He brings the final insult to you and every citizen in Gwinnett County, that the only explanation was he was framed, that he was framed."

"Well, let me ask. You saw Jack Burnette testify in this courtroom. You saw him on the videotape. You saw his pain. Would Jack Burnette frame Mike Chapel?"

According to Jack Burnette, that is precisely what happened. Burnette's Chapel Case Notes, page 20, 2:15 pm *(a) May Want to Manufacture Wit.* (Witnesses)

"What conceivable reason in the world would the Gwinnett County police department have to frame Michael Chapel? What possible explanation? Why Michael Chapel?"

Perhaps the cops that lost, destroyed, manipulated, stole, and manufactured evidence should be called to answer those questions?

"There is no explanation. There is no frame-up. The physical evidence doesn't support the frame-up theory, and the reasonable consequences don't form a frame-up theory."

Whether or not the frame-up was well reasoned seems irrelevant; the facts indicate that it did occur. The lead investigator was the lead man-ufacturer of evidence, and the lead prosecutor lied in open court. The lead prosecutor made shady deals to keep Bodie Hurst from running his mouth about whatever J. P. Morgan likely confessed to before executing his own guilty verdict and sentencing himself to death. It may be that for all his wrong-doing, Morgan tried to do the right thing on his way to meet his maker.

GCPD just was not interested in the truth, the leadership of GCPD was interested in convicting Michael Chapel, and they tried, in fact, to have him executed. He was getting too close. He had intel that implicated the wrong people or the criminals operating through GCPD were just too paranoid. Whatever the reason, GCPD decided that Chapel had to go, and they hoped to silence him forever.

Luke 12:2-3 But there is nothing carefully concealed that will not be revealed, and nothing secret that will not become known. Therefore, whatever you say in the darkness will be heard in the light, and what you whisper in private rooms will be preached from the rooftops.

Twenty-One

Juror #13 was ushered into the witness stand. Like other jurors, 63-year-old Phillip Sullivan was unnerved to find himself on an elevated platform questioned by Judge Bishop. He knew there must be turmoil within the jury pool.

"Mr. Sullivan," Judge Bishop began, *"I'd like to pose the following questions to you, and the first question is, at any time during the course of the trial of this case up to and including today, has any other juror suggested to you what the outcome of this case should be?"*

"No, sir," Sullivan said.

"Has any other... have you heard any other juror indicate that juror has made up his or her mind as to what the verdict, in this case, should be?"

"No."

"Has any other juror suggested to you what the verdict should be?"

"No."

"Thank you very much." The judge dismissed the juror, and Sullivan exited the courtroom as a dozen other jurors had done. Ten were asked the same questions Sullivan just answered.

"Your Honor," Porter addressed the court, *"I think we are caught in the horns of a dilemma. I don't know which one is not telling us the truth, but we've got somebody not telling us the truth."*

Why?

Because Juror #5, Daisy McAfee, had sent Judge Bishop a note saying, 'I need to talk to Judge Bishop concerning a very biased remark made to me concerning this case.'

The judge ordered the courtroom closed and brought in Juror McAfee to discuss the matter.

"All right, Ms. McAfee, would you tell me what the remark was?"

"It was a remark that I didn't think should be made to me," McAfee said, *"and I don't know if anybody else heard it, but the remark was 'I think the prosecution is railroading Chapel and has been all along, just because of one car that drove by and identified him.'"*

There was an audible gulp from the State's counsel table as Danny Porter realized he had a significant problem.

"And who made this remark to you?" Judge Bishop questioned, the prospect of a mistrial swirling anxiously in his head.

"That was Mr. Jim - I'm not sure what his last name is. He's the only one in there named Jim."

They identified Jim Knowlson as the person who allegedly remarked multiple times and discussed with yet another juror that the State, represented by the lead prosecutor, Danny Porter, was engaged in *"railroading"* Michael Chapel.

When Judge Bishop instructed McAfee to return to the Jury Pool and not speak of the situation or what was discussed, she asked Judge Bishop if she should lie to the other jurors about why she was taken from the pool.

"Just say nothing," Judge Bishop responded flatly. *"It's nobody else's business."*

Twenty-One

Knowlson was brought in next, and the judge asked if he had made such comments.

"Of course not," Knowlson said.

"All right," Bishop prodded, *"You've not made any suggestions in the presence of any other jurors that the - you feel like the defendant is being railroaded or any suggestions along those lines?"*

"No, Sir."

Bishop prodded, and Knowlson affirmed his impartiality and willingness to hear all the facts before deliberating guilt or innocence. Once the Judge was satisfied, he called the attorneys to the bench for a sidebar. Porter was not satisfied. He wanted Knowlson disqualified.

"I'm concerned as a factual matter that he has expressed an opinion to another juror," Porter said, *"and I'm going to - I move to excuse him at this point."*

"We'll do all that on the record in a minute," The Judge responded.

Porter would move in open court to disqualify Knowlson for fear he had already made up his mind. Porter argued that Ms. McAfee would have no reason to make up the comment and that it would so prejudice the jury.

Chapel's defense counsel objected to Knowlson's ejection. They said Knowlson was just as credible as McAfee and had affirmed that no such comment was made. Therefore, there was no reason to believe he could not remain fair and impartial.

The Judge expressed concern that disqualifying Knowlson would be considered a 'reversible error,' and he was, therefore, reticent to uphold Porter's motion. The judge decided to ask the rest of the jurors if such a comment was made, and one by one, each juror was brought in and asked the same questions by Judge Bishop. Each juror answered as had Phillip Sullivan: *"No, sir."*

McAfee had alleged that at least one Juror expressed an opinion to her and at least one other that Michael Chapel was being railroaded. The

State viewed this as a juror disqualification issue; the Court considered it a potentially reversible error. After every other juror denied hearing the allegations, the judge decided to do nothing.

The Judge overruled Porter's motion, and the trial continued toward its ignominious conclusion, with both Knowlson and McAfee firmly planted on the panel, even though one of them was lying.

One of those jurors, Phillip Sullivan, listened intently to all the evidence and took copious notes. Though Sullivan had not heard any comments about 'railroading' and had endeavored to reserve judgment until the end, he eventually became convinced that Chapel was innocent and would later coin the phrase the *Gwinnett County Railroad* as an ode to this case.

After the judge gave his final instructions to the panel, they were guided to the conference room, where they would deliberate. At this point, Sullivan was informed that he had been the alternate juror and would not join in the deliberations.

Sullivan hardly expected to have a significant impact on the jury's decision. They had all heard what he heard, they saw what he saw, and he expected that they, like him, could not in good conscience find Chapel guilty.

Still sequestered with the jury pool, Sullivan heard the voting tally from the first vote on the first day of deliberations. It was nine votes for acquittal and three votes for guilty. He was surprised it had not been unanimous for not guilty but figured the three guilty votes would come around to not guilty once they discussed the evidence or lack thereof.

When the empaneled jury returned to the jury box on the fifth day, virtually all red-faced and in tears, Sullivan thought, They couldn't possibly...

"*Mr. Foreman,*" Bishop asked, "*Have you reached a verdict?*"

"*Yes, sir,*" the jury foreman responded. "*I suppose we have.*"

Phillip Sullivan, a retired executive, and former military intelligence officer, who had played a critical role in the United States' response to the

Soviet militarization of East Berlin during the Cold War, stood in shock. Three consecutive guilty verdicts were read aloud in the Gwinnett County Superior Courtroom. Many in the courtroom and virtually everyone in the jury box was in tears. The prosecution team and Emogene Thompson's few attending family members expressed relieved jubilation.

Only Chapel and Sullivan stood in silence, no emotion visible on either face. The two men had never met. Sullivan knew Chapel only from the trial, though he felt as if he knew him at that moment. On the other hand, Chapel had heard Sullivan answer the judge's three questions with a total of four words and had no idea that Sullivan's absence from the deliberations would have such an impact on his life.

At that moment, however, Chapel had never been more desolate. His family and a small contingent of his friends knew he was innocent, and though they would have little success, they would crash themselves into rocks trying to get anyone to help them for the better part of the next three decades. Chapel had spent the last two and a half years in protective custody—perpetual lock down—as he awaited trial, and he would spend most of the next decade languishing in a 5'x 8' cell isolated from virtually all human contact.

Phillip Sullivan became incensed at the injustice he watched unfold. He had many unanswered questions but knew from the testimony presented that Chapel was not at the scene of the crime on the night in question. He understood investigations from his time in military intelligence, and he knew that there were many demonstrable problems with how the Emogene Thompson murder investigation had been conducted. Most of all, he was astonished by how poorly the defense team had performed.

Sullivan stewed over the case for a few days then decided to reach out to the defense team. He asked about their unwillingness to attack the problems with the prosecution's case that he considered most egregious.

He was able to contact Johnny Moore's co-counselor, Elizabeth Vila Rogan.

Sullivan asked why the defense had not attacked the prosecution's obvious obfuscation concerning the raincoat and the crime scene. Why did the defense not attack the prosecution over the loss of evidence: the dispatch tapes, intel files from Chapel's locker, phone records, or the destruction of the gun found at the Inn? Why did the defense team not challenge the prosecution concerning the alibi testimony of the Firemen? Why did they not attack the two police officers who had both changed their initial statements, falsified their log sheets, and admitted to lying?

"Those are some excellent points, Mr. Sullivan," Rogan said, "and I've shared them with Johnny. Hopefully, we'll be able to get Michael a new trial on appeal, and we'll utilize this material."

Sullivan was astounded by the defense team's response. With evidence to support his theory, he would ultimately conclude that Johnny Moore had worked, at least to some degree, in collusion with his old friend and colleague, Danny Porter.

However, he decided to wait and see if Chapel would fare better in the appeals process, as he believed there was much to appeal concerning this verdict. In the meantime, he wrote down everything he remembered from the trial while still fresh in his mind.

After monitoring the papers and the Internet for six months and seeing no action in the case, Phillip Sullivan decided to take action and devoted the rest of his time, energy, and a considerable portion of his retirement funds in pursuit of justice for a man he had not yet met – A man the State of Georgia now considered a convicted murderer.

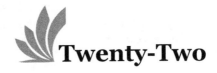

Twenty-Two

Sullivan began his March 1996 booklet, 'Justice – Has Justice Been Served? You Decide' with a letter he sent to Chapel: *"Dear Mr. Chapel, I was an alternate juror in your case and believe you to be innocent of the murder of Emogene Thompson. It is my opinion that your attorneys at the trial did not adequately represent you. I cannot advise you as to what you should do.*

Enclosed is an analysis of the defense in your trial that I feel could serve as a basis for an appeal, as well as some correspondence with your attorneys subsequent to your trial. With this, I feel that I have done everything that I can do to right your situation. All I can do now is to wish you good luck. Sincerely, Philip R. Sullivan."

What followed was a detailed scrutiny of much of the evidence used to convict Officer Chapel and the opening salvo in what would become Phillip Sullivan's life's work. Sullivan offered a twenty-five-subject breakdown beginning with an overview of the crime and initial investigation.

"The crime scene was of critical importance to the defense, but they seemed to pay little attention to it. When pictures of the crime scene, including the body of Mrs. Thompson, were published to the jury, Mr. Moore objected because they would only 'tend to inflame the jury.'"

"The testimony of the medical examiner was also critical to the defense, and again the defense seemed to pay little attention to this evidence."

Sullivan also pointed to numerous inconsistencies and holes in the theories presented by the Medical Examiner.

"There are huge holes in this theory, and the defense did not develop any of them. First, if the killer put his hand through the rear driver's side window, he would have been put-ting his hand through a closed window. Remember, accord-ing to the crime scene technicians, all the windows except the driver's window were intact and completely closed, and all the doors were locked."

"According to the prosecution's theory, the killer would have had to open the driver's door, which was found to be locked, unlock the back door, roll down the rear window, fire the shot, roll up the back window, re-lock the back door, and finally lock the driver's door."

"This scenario then shows a left-handed killer bias that totally contradicts the police and the prosecution's theory that Emogene Thompson's killer had to be right-handed. There is also strong presumption that the alleged police officer most probably asked for Mrs. Thompson's papers, causing her to turn away from the killer to reach into her glove compartment."

"Michael Chapel is right-handed, and it is difficult to believe that he would have asked Mrs. Thompson to produce any documents from the glove compartment of her automobile."

Sullivan poked hole after hole in the prosecution's case, relentlessly pointing out where the Defense team had failed to do the same. He made a point regarding the testimony of Karl Kautter and Paul Omodt. Sullivan would later be proven correct by scientific study.

"The driver, Mr. Olmut (Omodt), stated that he drove at the legal speed limit, 45 MPH, and did not stop for any stop signs during this entire period. Both wit-nesses stated that after driving parallel with them for the 45 seconds, the police car pulled ahead of them and turned right at Raymond H. Smith St."

"It is exactly seven-tenths (.7) of a mile from the Gwinnco Muffler Shop to Raymond H. Smith St. At 45 MPH without any intervening stops, that distance would take 64 seconds to traverse. Now, if the policeman they saw walking toward the car, walked up to, per-haps conversed with Mrs. Thompson and then killed her with two gunshots, retrieved her purse and then got back into his car,

caught up with the Kautter/Olmut vehicle, drove in tandem with them for 45 seconds and then passed them finally turning off on Raymond H. Smith, the time frame does not make sense."

What Kautter and Omodt testified to is impossible. Moreover, Kautter later came forward of his own volition through counsel to recant his testimony. He told another private investigator that the District Attorney's office had told him to lie and coached him on his testimony.

"Finally, testimony from the firefighters at the Precinct/Fire Station where the officers were between late afternoon and the time that they left, indicated that Officer Chapel donned only a raincoat when he left, and Officer Chapel's hat rain cover was recovered during a search of the Iron World Gym after his arrest."

"None of this was developed by the defense in cross-examination. Instead, they concerned themselves with the presence of another officer, Brian Reddy, at the Circle K convenience store about one mile away approximately at that time. Officer Reddy, who had reported his presence at that place on his police log, admitted that he lied about that entry, and he did not leave the fire station during the entire time frame."

"A much more reasonable scenario for the incident would be that the Kautter/Olmut automobile passed the Gwinnco Muffler Shop later than they stated after all the officers at the fire station had resumed their patrols. The Gwinnco Muffler Shop was in Officer Reddy's patrol area. And my guess is that they saw Officer Reddy in the Gwinnco Muffler driveway. On exiting his vehicle with a flashlight, he saw the flat left-front tire, decided the vehicle was disabled and temporarily abandoned, returned to his police car, resumed his patrol, catching up quickly with the Kautter/Omodt vehicle and so forth. Officer Reddy was never questioned about this, but given his reckless treatment of the truth, it is doubtful that he would have admitted it. Officer Reddy's picture should have been on that police photo lineup with Officer Chapel."

Sullivan's pamphlet would be passed out across Gwinnett County, and volunteers would face severe opposition from members of the Gwinnett County Police Department for distributing the literature.

One volunteer had numerous run-ins with Gwinnett County Police. The hard-working single mother of two, a Gwinnett County employee, school bus driver, was forcibly removed from multiple establishments where no complaint was lodged. At one point, an officer told her to be careful that she did not share in Chapel's fate. Inspired by Sullivan and incensed with Gwinnett County, she pressed forward undaunted and refused to give up the fight for Chapel's freedom. A battle she is still actively waging up to the time of this writing.

Sullivan became a certified private investigator and served as Chapel's lead investigator for years. He and Chapel produced countless court filings, solicited expert and scientific opinions, forensic analysis, and did the job GCPD, and Danny Porter refused to do.

Phillip Sullivan took Chapel's injustice to his grave. Mr. Sullivan passed away in 2013, leaving behind a road map to the truth and the legacy of an exemplary citizen willing to fight for truth and justice. Phillip R. Sullivan was the thirteenth juror who became the first armchair investigator turned professional investigator to uncover the facts of this case. There would be more.

Like Sullivan, Boris Korczak, Robert Korczak, Pamela Holcombe, Tom Conroy, Harold Chapel, and many others would take up the case of the State vs. Michael Harold Chapel and each would add to the body of evidence. All became convinced that the Danny Porter-led *Gwinnett County Railroad* first left the station in Spring 1993; its first victim Michael Harold Chapel. This book stands on their shoulders as a testament to their unwavering belief that in America, in the end, the truth must prevail.

 **Twenty-Three**

We have all heard the maxim: a person that represents himself in a court of law has a fool for a client. The legal profession requires a keen understanding of an ever-changing and shifting body of law and procedural etiquette. To gain this understanding requires years of research, study, and experience. Mistakes in practice, however, can literally cost you your freedom or even your life.

Before April 23, 1993, Michael Chapel never imagined that he needed criminal representation and never would have considered representing himself if facing criminal accusation, as he indeed found himself facing the worst charges imaginable on this date. Chapel, an experienced law enforcement officer, willingly submitted himself to interrogation by his superior officers and, in one case, a man he considered a friend and mentor. He proclaimed his innocence.

He provided his alibi that he knew, despite the misinformation being manufactured and fed to him, was legitimate and verifiable. Once he realized they intended to charge him with this heinous crime, he imagined he would have to defend himself for a short time. He was to be incarcerated with an inmate population that he was nearly forty percent responsible for arresting. Still, upon making bail, he was confident that he would be able to go about proving his innocence.

His bail was set at $500,000.00, burdened with unusual restrictions placed on his bail application. It changed multiple times arbitrarily in an effort that denied him the opportunity to investigate the circumstances surrounding the accusations against him. Undaunted, Chapel began to connect with his various confidants and fellow officers who wanted to help him prove his innocence.

As he and his newly employed legal representative, Walt Britt, Esquire, began poking gaping holes in the prosecution's soon-to-be Swiss cheese case, Chapel remained cut off from access to the phone at the jail where he was housed. Kept in protective custody – 23-hours-a-day solitary confinement – and allowed to discuss his case only once a week when Walt Britt came to discuss his defense.

Multiple employees from that period have expressed concern over the treatment of Chapel that they describe as a concerted effort to keep Chapel isolated and depressed. Footage of Chapel's family members, particularly his brother, a Gwinnett County Sheriff Deputy, tearfully pleading for Chapel's life, was played on a loop outside Chapel's cell.

Medical staff were instructed not to render aid or comfort to Chapel, including the instruction not to provide him with Tylenol if requested. A nurse from the jail describes the circumstances of Chapel's treatment as dire. In her opinion, a concerted effort to provoke Chapel to commit violence against himself or others, something she came to believe, was impossible for a man of Chapel's character.

Once Walt Britt was removed from his case, Chapel was utterly at the mercy of a system that presumed his guilt at a roadside tribunal. A system that charged and arraigned him and publicly declared him guilty two and a half years before the trail. A system that denied him defense counsel of his choosing.

Michael Chapel was the bad guy; the system was sure of it. But Britt was a foil to the system's plans of wrapping up a high-pressure case and ridding the department of a crusading cop that was unpopular with a particular clique within the department.

Britt, a well-connected and highly successful Gwinnett County-based defense attorney, was punching holes in the 'airtight' case and discovering new evidence through his private investigation efforts. This made Britt the only effective counsel Chapel had during his twenty-eight years of prosecution and incarceration.

The Georgia Supreme Court would ultimately agree that Johnny Moore, Britt's successor, provided ineffective counsel. According to the Justices and pursuant to its former precedence of disallowing cumulative error to trigger verdict nullification, the ineffective counsel by itself was not considered enough to overturn the verdict and order a new trial. They recognized ineffective counsel that was outside of the control of the defendant.

The Police Defense Foundation, a fledgling Washington DC based non-profit, heard about Chapel's case from Congressman James Traficant, who had conducted his own armchair investigation. Convinced that Chapel was an innocent man, Traficant asked the foundation to take up the case. Attorney Randy Mott, an environmental attorney, was assigned to handle Chapel's appeal. Mott had limited experience as counsel for the defense.

Mott, along with former CIA double agent to the KGB, Boris Korczak, and his son Robert Korczak, a former congressional aide to Traficant, signed up as investigators and completed the defense team for the 1997 Appeal before the State of Georgia's Supreme Court. The new defense team descended on Gwinnett County, held a press conference to bring Chapel's case back into the public consciousness, and immediately faced fierce opposition from District Attorney Danny Porter, as well as the GCPD, and some in the press.

Porter ridiculed and mocked Mott publicly, calling him a charlatan seeking donations and notoriety for the Police Defense Foundation. Boris, a perceptive and experienced espionage operative, noted a surveillance team marking their every move in Georgia. The District Attorney followed, threatened, and mocked the defense team in the press.

Robert Korczak described the day that the defense team was leaving the hotel to appear, on Chapel's behalf, in front of the State's Supreme Court in Atlanta.

"Gwinnett County Police cars lined up from the exit of the hotel, down the road leading to I-85 and virtually bumper to bumper from where we got on the interstate and all the way to Spaghetti-Junction (Interstate transition from several major highways and interstates.)," Korczak recalled. "They all parked on the side of the road, with their blue lights flashing. Most of the officers were just standing next to their vehicles, looking at us as we passed. It was clear they were giving us a show of force."

Mott corroborated Korczak's description and added, "When we entered or exited our hotel room, two or three guys were staying in the rooms adjacent to us, that were always wearing flak jackets and tactical gear. They made a point to appear in their doorways and usually followed us in such an obvious manner that they could only be attempting to intimidate us." Mott also acknowledged that he gravely underestimated the opposition Chapel was facing and apologized to Chapel and his family for being in over his head.

"I really failed him," Mott told Storied Press in December of 2020 on a Skype video call.

"I did the best I could, but I had no idea going in, just how far the prosecution had gone and was willing to go to twist and distort the facts. Michael needed a more experienced criminal defense team, familiar with the Georgia Judiciary, and the Police Defense Foundation just wasn't able to afford that."

Mott's appeal was denied, and Michael lost the ability to appeal many of the aspects of the trial that were in legal error. Mott left the legal profession and currently runs a green energy business in Poland. He cites this case and Danny Porter's tactics as significant reasons for his life-altering decisions.

Another non-profit, the Georgia Innocence Project, recommended Kevin Steel as an attorney, and Steel would accept $5,000 from H. L. Chapel, Michael's father, to prepare and file a motion with the Georgia Supreme Court for DNA testing. Mike had been working on such a motion for years and had prepared a layman's draft that was provided to Steel for reference.

Steel removed Chapel's cover page, replaced it with a cover of his own, and filed the motion as written by Chapel, sans proofing. In effect, the ineffective appellate counsel fortified the ineffective trial counsel, and

Twenty-Three

Chapel quickly ran out of avenues to seek justice through the courts.

In retrospect, it appears that you only get one real bite at the apple. It is legal doctrine, and if your defense counsel is not up to the task, and the prosecution is willing to poison the apple tree, you may find yourself locked away for the better part of three decades pleading with appellate courts extremely hesitant to hear the pleas of a convicted felon.

Michael Chapel had two choices. He could face the cold reality that he had been convicted and would have little or no assistance in seeking justice. Or he could educate himself in the law, immerse himself in the facts of the case, and fight the insurmountable odds to keep hope alive for his family and a small handful of friends and supporters that knew the truth.

Chapel is still fighting. He became a certified paralegal, has done decades of legal research, and with the help of a small collection of dedicated investigators and his loving family, has preserved the record of truth in the case of the State of Georgia v. Michael Harold Chapel. Chapel became his own best defense counsel, not because he has a fool for a client, but because he was left with no other choice.

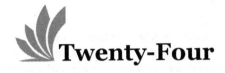

Twenty-Four

"*Your Honor, my name is Michael Chapel, and I am the Petitioner in this case.*"

By the year 2006, Chapel had tried in futility, for well over a decade, to rely on the justice system to provide him with a fair trial, a fair appeals process when that failed, or any fair finding of facts. Chapel had been through numerous trial lawyers, investigators, and legal aids, and all had fallen short and proven ineffective for various reasons.

In his desperation, Chapel determined the only way he would have hope of a proper defense was if he provided it for himself, though the venues to make his case had dwindled to almost nothing. Chapel prepared and filed a motion put before the Georgia Supreme Court. In March 2006, the Court ruled in his favor, and oral arguments were ordered for June of the same year.

When it became apparent that inmate Chapel was preparing to make arguments in his own defense, the Supreme Court preemptively remanded the case back to the original trial court – the Superior Court of Gwinnett County.

Chapel's opening statement began...

"*On the night of April 23, 1993, I was arrested and charged with a crime I did not commit, the murder of Emogene Thompson on the night of April 15th of that year. In September of 1995, a jury convicted me of the murder of Mrs. Thompson, and in September of 1998, the Supreme Court of Georgia denied my direct appeal."*

"The Judicial system of the State of Georgia has set seemingly impossible barriers when a prisoner attempts to move from the criminal justice system to that of the civil, habeas corpus system. Rulings have been that issues raised in direct appeal cannot be again raised in habeas corpus, and issues not raised in direct appeal are automatically deemed to have been waived. This is quite different from the Federal system toward which the Georgia State Legislature has urged the Courts to move."

"This 'catch-22' position would seem to preclude any successfully valid habeas corpus actions in this state, and yet this is certainly not the case. In order to establish the exception then, a petitioner would have to prove 1) that issues brought in direct appeal were brought without proof or were otherwise empty, or 2) that issues brought in habeas are substantially different than those previously brought in direct appeal, and 3) that issues not brought in direct appeal could not have been brought at the time, because, in fact, they were unknown to me."

"These are precisely the issues and effects of the case I bring before you." Chapel continued, and then he presented a case with direct evidence of *"massive prosecutorial misconduct, ineffective assistance of counsel and apparent collusion"* between the Prosecutor and his own defense counsel.

Chapel puts before the court that his bond was not only excessive, at $500,000.00, but the Sheriff of Gwinnett County, Georgia placed arbitrary conditions on that bond that made it impossible for friends and family to raise the amount needed. Chapel was incarcerated, isolated in protective custody, and unable to assist in his defense. All of which violated the Eighth and Fourteenth Amendments to the United States Constitution and similar guarantees under the Constitution of the State of Georgia.

Chapel was deprived of his constitutional right and expressed the desire for a speedy trial as guaranteed under the Sixth and Fourteenth Amendments to the United States Constitution and similar guarantees under the Constitution of the State of Georgia.

"This violation resulted from a ploy to delay my trial by the District Attorney of

Gwinnett County, while he combed the jails and prisons of Georgia in search of witnesses against me, sending the case to the Supreme Court of Georgia with a tangential issue: that my defense counsel, Walt Britt, knew too much about the workings of Gwinnett County government, and then transferring litigation to the right of choice of counsel, a non-issue that had been settled months before."

Indeed, if Walt Britt had a conflict of interest representing Chapel, the conflict existed on the day Chapel's family retained Britt to represent him. The District Attorney did not challenge Britt's right to represent Chapel for nearly a year constituted acceptance. Moreover, the Judge accepted Britt as trial counsel.

The District Attorney waited for an opportune situation, which he knew to be inevitable before he acted. He knew the Chapel's funds were limited and that he would eventually have to appeal to the State for assistance in attorney fees and other legal expenses.

He also knew that the County's Solicitor General would take up the issue of Chapel's employment with the county and coordinated his attacks with the Solicitor.

The District Attorney succeeded with delaying tactics in the case until he was able to maneuver things to have a defense attorney appointed to defend Chapel that was more to his liking.

Johnny Moore, the Attorney appointed by Judge Bishop, was familiar to Porter as the two had spent years working together as Assistant District Attorneys. It is believed that Moore hired young Danny Porter into the District Attorney's office. It is also believed that Porter recommended Moore to Judge Bishop for this case.

"My trial, in August and September of 1995, was fundamentally biased and unfair in violation of my rights under the 'due process clause' of the Fifth and Fourteenth Amendments of the United States Constitution and like guarantees under the Constitution of the State of Georgia." Chapel argued.

"My trail was fraught with prosecutorial misconduct and ineffective assistance of counsel to the extent that there was apparent collusion between the District Attorney of Gwinnett County, Danny Porter, and Lead Defense Counsel, Johnny Moore, and possibly other counsel on both sides."

Michael Chapel

The extensive nature of the prosecutorial misconduct and ineffective assistance of counsel became apparent to researchers, including Phillip Sullivan, an alternate juror at the 1995 trial. Sullivan made a startling connection while researching the documents for Ground Twelve - Prosecutorial Misconduct, and Ground Fifteen - Ineffective Assistance of Defense Counsel. The two grounds seemed a mirrored reflection of each other as if choreographed.

Ground Sixteen in Chapel's filing documents the instances of apparent collusion between the District Attorney and Defense Counsel. More than thirteen instances of coordination or collusion are presented.

"The evidence presented to the jury did not support the guilty verdict in my case. This contention is documented in Ground Five of my petition. There is no question that there was some sort of law enforcement vehicle in the driveway of Gwinnco Muffler on the night of the murder. Witness statements and testimony place a so-called 'mystery police car' in the driveway facing out toward Peachtree Industrial Boulevard as early as 8:45 PM and as late as 9:30 PM. However, witness testimony by all accounts places me at Firehouse 14 during that entire period." Chapel continued.

"In his closing argument, Porter disputed this by stating that three people stated I left the firehouse at or about 9:30 PM. Sergeant Donald Stone, Officer Brian Reddy, and Firefighter David Pierce, most bizarre."

Sergeant Stone testified at trial that Chapel left the firehouse between 9:20 and 9:30 pm. His testimony was impeached by his statement to Captain Davis shortly after the murder that he (Stone) left the Firehouse about 20 minutes after Chapel to call his wife. That call occurred from the precinct at 10:17 pm, exactly twenty-one minutes after the dispatch call sending Chapel to the Arden Road call. Unbelievably, Defense Counsel Johnny Moore did not confront Stone with the evidence of the telephone call during the prosecution phase.

The jury heard later only that Sgt. Stone had made a telephone call, but they had no information about when Stone made that call nor told Captain Davis that he left the firehouse twenty minutes after Chapel in connection to that call.

Twenty-Four

Firefighter Pierce could only relate that Chapel had left the firehouse at the conclusion of a movie. At the prodding of the District Attorney and with the help of a TV Guide, Pierce thought the movie was a feature on cable, which had ended at 9:30 pm.

This testimony contradicted the other first responders, who, like Chapel, testified that they were watching a network broadcast movie and that movie ended at 10 pm. It was also noted that neither GCPD nor the District Attorney's office interviewed the firemen until just before the trial, nearly two and a half years after the night in question.

"Even more incomprehensible was that during my interrogation, I said at one point that I had left the firehouse about 9:30 PM." Chapel acknowledged. *"I do not remember saying this, and I have no idea what could have prompted me to say this, but prompted I must have been, either by the interrogator or by one of the police officers and others just outside of that tiny interrogation room."*

Chapel had no way of knowing at the time that Latty, Burnette, and the leadership of GCPD had met prior to his interrogation and strategized precisely how to get Chapel to incriminate himself, in addition to 'manufacturing witnesses,' we learn from Burnette's handwritten notes that the interrogators intended to 'feed Chapel the facts' to have him make statements they could use against him.

The statement occurred at the end of the interrogation as Chapel was being arrested. Burnette and Latty, even more so, had been 'feeding him the facts' all night and trying to insert their version of events, including the impossible timeline. Chapel truthfully told the interrogators several times during the interview that he left the firehouse around the time that he received the dispatch call to Arden Drive at 2156 (9:56 pm).

When Chapel made this statement to his interrogators, his world was collapsing. He would be arrested for a heinous crime that he did not commit. He would be ripped away from his wife and children – his life. Lt. Latty, the chief interrogator, was railing at him about God and religion and how his soul could yet be saved. It is not hard to imagine Chapel tuning out and erroneously repeating a time fed to him countless times over the last several hours. Chapel's departure time discrepancy should have been the most verifiable event that occurred on April 15, 1993.

Chapel, the firemen, and D. E. Stone (in his original statement) put Chapel at the firehouse until nearly 2200 (10:00 PM), meaning that he would have been, as he claims, in the firehouse day room at 2156 when Dispatch queued him on the chronologically recorded police radio. The day room at the firehouse is equipped with a speaker that is constantly squawking the chronologically recorded fire department radio traffic into the day room.

If Chapel was approximately fourteen inches from the speaker while responding to Police Dispatch, as he claims, then the recording of that call would have captured the fire traffic as background noise and would be easily verifiable. Lt. John Latty checked out those dispatch tapes. According to his testimony at trial, he listened to them once and "lost" the recordings.

Moreover, Chapel's 2207 to 2211 arrival to Arden Road and subsequent activity at said call, some fifteen minutes away from the murder scene, presented a significant problem for Porter. Chapel's presence at the scene is virtually impossible before 2240 or later, well after the window of death and long after the witnesses described the six-foot, medium-built officer at the scene.

Porter's timeline called for Chapel to be on the scene by 2145. Although, his timeline does not explain the existence of the cop at the scene as early as 2045 and continuously until 2130.

Ground Six of Chapel's filing documents Porter's attempts to manipulate witness testimony and to plant false memories in their minds.

All the witnesses to the blue light activity in the driveway of Gwinnco Muffler did give an estimate of the time in which they passed the muffler shop that seemed to support Porter's contention of 2145. In every instance, the remainder of witness testimony supported a time of 2200 (10:00 pm) or later when they drove past the crime scene.

 **Twenty-Five**

Witness Daniel Gravitt gave the most accurate estimate of the time of the blue light activity. Although he gave an earlier time, Gravitt testified that he was on his way to pick up his daughter from a babysitting gig at a location he estimated five minutes from the muffler shop. He further testified that he arrived at the babysitting location "shortly after 10 pm."

He waited a few minutes for his daughter and estimated another five minutes to the muffler shop on his way home, re-passing Gwinnco at 10:15 pm.

For other witnesses, the weather becomes the clock. When Gravitt passed the muffler shop, he describes a terrible storm raging, verified by local weather tracking, a sheeting downpour so heavy that he testifies only to see the reflection of the blue lights off the sheets of rain.

Paul Omodt, the driver of the Omodt/Kautter car, testified that the storm did not let up until they reached the intersection of Peachtree Industrial Boulevard and North Price Road. By the time they passed the muffler shop, the rain had slowed to a drizzle, indicating that when Gravitt passed Gwinnco Muffler, Omodt and Kautter were south of North Price Road.

Additionally, Omodt saw the blue lights from the top of a hill. However, by the time he and Kautter passed Gwinnco, the blue lights had been turned off.

Witness Alan Robertson also passed the muffler shop after Gravitt; this had to be true because the weather had cleared sufficiently for him to see detail on the victim's automobile in his rear-view mirror at a distance of 500 to 600 feet.

In an unsigned statement given to Lt. Latty, Harlan Preston stated that he left Duluth, 12 ½ miles from the crime scene, and reached the muffler shop after only ten to fifteen minutes. During the best conditions and speeding, that drive might take only fifteen minutes, but on the night of the murder when he left Duluth, that drive would have taken at minimum five minutes longer because of the storm. This would have Preston passing by the crime scene at 10:00 pm or later.

Like Preston, David McGaha left his workplace in Duluth, only five minutes earlier than Preston. Since McGaha's drive was similar to that of Preston, he would have passed the muffler shop at approximately 9:55 pm. He testified that only the victim's car was present in the driveway when he went past.

The statements of Amy Parker and Keith Seay, both neighbors of the victim, given to Jack Burnette on April 16, 1993, indicated that the victim left her home at 9:50 pm, her usual departure for work in Norcross. The muffler shop was 1.7 miles from the victim's driveway, and we now know that the flat front left tire was slashed before arrival at the muffler shop. This would validate McGaha's testimony of the victim's arrival – presumably in distress from a flat tire – just before 9:55 pm.

Ron Flashner's statement to Jack Burnette indicates another car had arrived on the scene 'a little before 10:00 pm.'

Flashner indicated that it was raining. A massive cloud of engine smoke engulfed the roadway making it impossible for him to positively identify the three or four individuals he saw around the victim's car. He described a big car backed up (trunk to truck) to the victim's car, facing Peachtree Industrial Boulevard.

Aside from ignoring the presence of these three or four individuals in a car that uniquely matched the description of Michael Thompson's

1978 Buick with a busted head gasket, the District Attorney had another problem. Witnesses Omodt and Kautter were the only witnesses to see the alleged officer in the driveway out of his vehicle. Both described the officer as about six feet tall with a medium build. Chapel is nearly six-foot-seven, 287 lbs. of solid muscle.

The District Attorney attempted to prove to the jury that the officer in the driveway returned to his vehicle. He tried to show that after walking up to the victim's darkened vehicle with a flashlight, unholstering his weapon and firing two fatal gunshots. Both shots were heard a half-mile away but not by the witnesses less than 500 feet away.

He was next to the victim's car when Omodt and Kautter passed. Chapel allegedly caught up to the Omodt/Kautter vehicle traveling approximately forty-five miles per hour within the time it took their vehicle to reach the two to four-lane transition that began just some 500 feet north of the Gwinnco Muffler driveway.

The officer in the driveway would have had to return to his vehicle, get in, back on to Peachtree Industrial Boulevard, then transition the car to drive and catch the Omodt/Kautter vehicle within the transition distance. This feat would require some sort of teleportation device.

To mislead the witness, the Court, and the jury, the District Attorney called Karl Kautter to describe the incident using a diagram that did not contain the driveway of the Gwinnco Muffler Shop. The image hid from the witness, Court, and jury the proximity of the muffler shop driveway to the two-to-four-lane transition of Peachtree Industrial Boulevard.

This proof of prosecutorial misconduct also proved ineffective assistance of counsel and the collusion of the District Attorney with Defense Counsel Johnny Moore. Moore stipulated to the use of that diagram and allowed this impossible timeline of events to be introduced virtually without objection.

Witness Kautter clearly did not understand the diagram and simply could do nothing but what he was instructed, even though he seemed skeptical of the distances.

When Prosecutor Porter asked witness Kautter to show the jury where the police car came up behind the pair that night, he replied, "Gwinnco Muffler would be approximately in here somewhere, and there's another building here." He said, pointing to a spot on the map close to the transition point.

"Well, Mr. Kautter, it's already been stipulated that Gwinnco Muffler is off the diagram to the south," Porter replied, pointing to some unknown spot off the map.

"Back that far?" Kautter seemed puzzled.

"Back that far." Porter insisted.

It is unknown what Porter was pointing to, but Photo Exhibit 6 – Peachtree Industrial Boulevard Going North – shows the impossibility of the police vehicle that passed the Omodt/Kautter car being the same vehicle the pair saw in the driveway of Gwinnco Muffler just seconds before.

Therefore, the only way Kautter and Omodt's testimony is plausible is if there was a second police vehicle that passed them at the point Peachtree Industrial Boulevard transitioned from two to four lanes.

In either event, at the time a police vehicle was passing the Omodt/Kautter vehicle, Chapel was at or near his assigned call on Arden Drive.

The District Attorney's next problem was that the autopsy, crime scene reports, and photographs proved that the shots that killed Emogene Thompson were fired from inside her vehicle.

The autopsy report describes two gunshot wounds to the victim's head. The first shot was described as a near contact wound that entered the victim's neck two inches below the left ear and exited through the extreme right of the victim's right eye socket. The shot splintered the lens in her glasses' right frame and deposited them onto the hump on the floor just under the console.

The second shot entered the victim's skull high and toward the rear of the victim's head, 62 inches from bottom (of heel) and exiting at the midline of the right temple.

To establish that the shots were fired from outside the vehicle as alleged, the District Attorney had to reverse the order of the shots to make any sense at all. He could not overcome the fact that the shot would have been from an unreasonable, downward angle.

Another problem with the scenario and the theory of the case presented to the jury by the prosecutor is the lack of blood spatter in the automobile.

There was virtually no blood spatter in the automobile. There was no blood spatter or even blood droplets on or around the driver's door where expected back spray would land. It would be practically impossible for high-velocity blood spatter to reach a raincoat outside the vehicle if, in contrast, there is no spatter anywhere in the pathway between the body and the bullet's origin.

Moreover, only a few low-velocity blood droplets were on the front passenger door where the high-velocity spatter should have been. If shot one had been the second shot, one would have expected to find the victim's glasses and glass shards on the passenger seat. Instead, blood spatter was found on the front floor hump in front of the console in the middle of the automobile.

Shot one could not have been accomplished from outside of the automobile. The doors were all locked, and only the driver's side window was partially open. Shot one could only have been fired from the left-back seat of the victim's vehicle, more than likely by a left-handed shooter or a person using his left hand due to the position of the seats. This is supported not only by the position of the victim's glasses but by the only occurrence of high-velocity blood spatter in the vehicle, on the vehicle's front windshield as described in the crime scene report and shown in Photo Exhibit 5-4.

Interestingly, the photograph of the front windshield of the victim's vehicle taken from outside of the vehicle was never shown to the jury when introduced into evidence. Instead, the photograph was misidentified by Office Ed Byers.

Instead of having the crime scene technician who snapped the picture and knew what she depicted in the image testify, it was successfully hidden from the jury, even though a jury member asked explicitly to see the photograph.

Again, the Defense counsel ignored this error and allowed the deceit to stand without objection. Yet again proving the intersection of prosecutorial misconduct with ineffective assistance of counsel, and thus another instance of probable collusion.

According to the prosecution, Michael Chapel was in dire straits financially. An issue was raised of Chapel spending $600.00 to pay for tee-shirts for the gym previously ordered and customary business expense. A $100 bill was used to pay for a car wash, and $139 was paid for a cash bond. The bond was paid in small denominations following a pass the hat collection by partygoers to bail out one of Eren Chapel's co-workers arrested after a rowdy birthday party. The car wash employee originally stated that the discounted car wash was paid with a $20 bill.

Porter became desperate to place more money in the hands of the Chapels once it became apparent that defense witness Jack Dudley would testify to issuing a $1,500 loan to Chapel. Dudley testified he provided the loan as an investment in the gym and was specifically earmarked to purchase tee shirts and other items that would be resold at the gym.

The funds for the loan had been drawn from the same bank where Dudley, the Chapels, and Emogene Thompson held accounts.

In the lead-up to the 1995 trial, a new witness, Kendon Curtis, appeared. Curtis claimed to be rifling through Eren Chapel's purse, apparently looking for something to steal, and saw an envelope containing $3,000 in $100 bills. While some of Eren Chapel's party members were in a convenience store and she was on the payphone, he was alone with the purse. He had time to count out precisely $3,000 but not enough time to steal it.

Eren Chapel's tip envelope was kept in her purse. It likely had four or five hundred dollars in small denominations, keeping with most cocktail and food service waitresses. GCPD had numerous opportunities to search Eren Chapel immediately after Chapel's arrest. They could have confiscated her purse, tip envelope, and any denominations of cash she may have had on her person, in her home, or her automobile. GCPD was

Twenty-Five

incurious about Eren Chapel's tip money until nearly two years later, after Dudley was listed as a defense witness and Danny Porter read the 'Powell Report.'

This incident highlights yet another act of probable collusion between the District Attorney and the Lead Defense Counsel. Johnny Moore and co-counsel Elizabeth Rogan persuaded Eren Chapel not to testify in rebuttal to the Kendon Curtis testimony.

Eren Chapel was perfectly willing to testify, incensed by the lies of Curtis and indignant that the prosecution was trying to use her meager hard-earned wages as a bludgeon against her husband. Eren Chapel was, in fact, insistent that she be allowed to set the record straight concerning Curtis nefariously attempting to gain access to her purse and tip money. Moore and Rogan dissuaded her and assured Eren and Michael Chapel that they had a strategy to deal with Curtis' lies. Apparently, the strategy was to just ignore it and let it stand.

Twenty-Six

There were three grounds for Chapel's arrest on the night of April 23, 1993, one week after the murder of Emogene Thompson. First, he had contact with the victim and her son in the two weeks before the murder. Second, hearsay statements from friends of the victim indicated that they spoke to Emogene Thompson about Chapel's so-called efforts to retrieve the $7,000.00 stolen from her trailer, probably by her son Michael.

Finally, two witnesses identified Chapel as both the driver of the 'mystery' patrol car that was in the Gwinnco Muffler driveway facing outward toward Peachtree Industrial Boulevard during the period from 2045 to 2130 and the driver of the patrol car that passed the Omodt/Kauter vehicle just north of the Gwinnco Muffler driveway. Despite an overwhelming media blitz to reinforce this narrative within days of Chapel's arrest, these grounds all began to fall apart shortly after Chapel's arrest.

On April 27, 1993, three days after Chapel's arrest, several firefighters who had been present in the firehouse on the night in question provided unsolicited statements to their Captain stating that Chapel had been at the firehouse from 2030 to 2200 or later. This concrete alibi made it impossible for Chapel to be at the crime scene at any time during the window of death or during the witnessed events of the evening. Now, investigators only had the statement of Officer Brian Reddy that allowed Chapel a sliver of time to have been at the scene.

Reddy admitted to lying, changed his story, lied on his log sheet, lied about possessing a weapon that matched the description of the murder weapon, and admitted to regularly lying about his police work.

The hearsay evidence of the victim's friends resulted from one of the two contacts Chapel had with the victim. The first contact resulted from Chapel's assignment to a report of theft at the victim's home. On arrival, Chapel determined that half of the $14,000.00 the victim kept at her home was missing. It was evident to Chapel that the son was the culprit.

Michael Thompson, the victim's son, had taken several hundred dollars from the stash, had a criminal background and a drug addiction, and no burglar in the history of humankind had ever taken only half of any find. Chapel told the victim his suspicion, confronted the son, and urged him to return his mother's money.

Since the apparent thief was her son, the victim declined to press the issue or file charges. Chapel reported the same to dispatch, and within minutes, briefed his supervisor, Sergeant Stone.

Stone recommended that Chapel write a report, despite no charges. Chapel complied and began to fill out the report on the incident but did not complete it. The incomplete report was later found in Chapel's briefcase. The second contact occurred the next day when the victim called the Northside Precinct and asked for Chapel. Sergeant Winderweedle took the call and left a message for Chapel. When Chapel came on duty, he tried to return the call, but there was no answer. Chapel stopped by the victim's home during shift. Emogene Thompson still did not want to prosecute her son but asked Chapel to help her. She reminded him that he had helped one of her friends with a daughter that stole her expensive jewelry.

Chapel related a police technique, known as 'the Boo,' that was successful in similar cases, including the friend's case. If she could successfully bluff her son into thinking that she was working with Chapel to recover the money, he was the prime suspect subject to imminent arrest when any evidence was found. The son might be scared and coerced into returning the money.

The complicated scheme was related to Emogene Thompson for only a few minutes while the two stood on her front porch. The hearsay statements from friends show every indication that either she or the friends or both misunderstood some or all of the plan. Thompson and her friends began to romanticize the plan to where Thompson became flattered that this 'good-looking cop' seemed interested in her. "He was (allegedly) following her around to protect her, and the two of them were planning a meeting."

The only other contact Chapel had with the family was with the son. Chapel was near his place of employment, a short time after the second meeting with Emogene Thompson. Chapel reinforced the Boo and again urged him to do the right thing and give his mother back her money.

There is no evidence of any other communications with either the victim or her son. The phone records from the victim's home and office, Chapel's home, gym, and precinct were all examined, as well as Chapel's intra-department communications channels.

Despite GCPD's best efforts, the Prosecutor could not establish any further communications with the victim and was left to opine that Chapel must have established and engaged in his plan for a clandestine meeting, eleven days in advance.

The third grounds for arrest were the witness identifications of the mystery cop. Dr. Robert Brusie, a veterinarian, passed the muffler shop driveway at 8:45 PM while the mystery police vehicle sat facing Peachtree Industrial Boulevard. Karl Kautter passed the muffler shop after 10:00 pm and was quickly overtaken just north of Gwinnco Muffler shortly after the blue lights of the police vehicle in the driveway were turned off. The identifications were made from a biased eight-photo lineup in which Chapel was the only officer from the Northside Precinct portrayed and thus unfairly highlighted.

At trial, Dr. Brusie, who picked Chapel as one of two possible matches, did remember that some months earlier, he had met Chapel at an accident scene when a horse was hit by a vehicle and had to be humanely destroyed. This allowed for the distinct possibility that Brusie recognized Chapel from the previous incident and not from Gwinnco. Moreover, when Dr. Brusie passed the muffler shop, Chapel was at the firehouse by all accounts.

Michael Chapel

Kautter's identification of Chapel was even more dubious and could only be described as confused at best. At one point, Kautter mentioned Officer J. P. Morgan, unprompted. Morgan, the officer who committed suicide shortly after being named by the defense as the likely ringleader of a set-up scheme to frame Chapel, did fit the description both Kautter and Omodt related to police. Approximately six-foot, medium build.

Since Kautter identified an officer at the muffler shop, he and Omodt could not possibly have seen the same officer seconds later passing them some 500 feet from the Gwinnco Muffler driveway. Therefore, his Identification of Chapel as driver of a second police car would have been exculpatory.

In retrospect, it is no surprise that Buford and Sugar Hill residents knew Chapel's face. Chapel was the only officer permanently assigned to the City of Buford at the request of Buford City officials. It would have been surprising if these folks had not seen Chapel driving a patrol car around these cities. It was well established that both Brusie and Kautter had previously encountered Officer Chapel during his police work for GCPD.

Ultimately, the grounds for Chapel's arrest begin to collapse on the very night of his arrest, in fact before his arrest, when Brian Reddy admitted that he was lying and that Chapel was at the firehouse as Chapel had claimed.

The collective response to the exonerating developments quickly evolved into an intentional conspiracy to convict Chapel of the crime, regardless of compelling evidence to the contrary. A crime that all key players should have realized Chapel was not involved in.

Eventually, it would be clear that this conspiracy involved high-ranking officials of the Gwinnett County Police Department, the District Attorney's office, the District Attorney himself, a Georgia State Crime Lab member, and finally and most unbelievably, Chapel's own defense counsel.

To convict Chapel, this Gwinnett County Cabal constructed a web of lies, deceit, corruption, and betrayal amongst the rank and file. They used their power to coerce the police department and other vestiges of county government, as well as a deadly wielding of the media narrative that was meticulously weaved and closely controlled by famed publicity hound Danny Porter and his understudy at the police department, Steve Cline.

They managed to taint the court of public opinion sufficiently and then so confused the jury that many of them ultimately voted for guilt with the belief that Chapel would win an appeal. Christopher Ford, one such juror reported to the press after trial, "None of us understood what was going on, it was like somebody put a blindfold on us or something." The jury never had a chance.

Why would these otherwise accomplished and respectable people enter such a dreadful conspiracy? Why not simply release Chapel back to duty, duly investigate the murder and bring the true culprits to justice?

The upside to convicting a highly commended and popular street cop would assure their futures and allow their stars to rise. That is precisely what did happen.

In the Gwinnett County Police Department, Assistant Chief White became Chief of Police White. Captain Davis would eventually follow White and became Chief of Police Davis. Lt. Latty went on to become Captain Latty and, shortly after that, Assistant Chief Latty.

Sergeant Cline quickly became Lt. Cline and shortly Captain Cline. Investigator Burnette retired from the GCPD and went to work for the district attorney's office as Lead Investigator Burnette the next day. ADA Scott Smeal went on to the State Attorney General's office. Danny Porter was re-elected district attorney of Gwinnett County and served in that capacity for twenty-eight years, citing the Chapel case as career-defining.

Johnny Moore became qualified to defend capital cases in the State of Georgia. He also appeared to be the go-to appointee in high-profile cases for Gwinnett County, sort of the judicial equivalent of the Washington Generals. An automatic win for the Danny Porter show.

On the other hand, had these people made the difficult decision to admit their mistake, people would have been acutely embarrassed and in jeopardy of witnessing the ignominious end of their careers.

They recognized the real possibility of municipal and civil lawsuits for false arrest, false imprisonment, deprivation of civil rights, defamatory, slander, and ultimately the conspiracy that would have engulfed them all.

Gwinnett County, GCPD, and specifically Lt. John Latty were burned shortly before the Chapel case with another case involving false arrest, libelous, and slander. Gwinnett County was forced to settle that case for a reported ten million dollars.

On numerous occasions, Lt. Latty also claimed that he had a special relationship with God, relating that he was placed in his position by God to bring to justice those evildoers as identified to him by God himself. Once God identified Chapel to Latty, he could not be deterred by a silly thing like not having any evidence whatever. Chapel was the evildoer. God himself had revealed it to Latty.

Predictably, the trial court in Gwinnett County denied Chapel's motion on a technicality, and no evidentiary review was conducted. The denial was upheld on appeal to the State Supreme Court, and Michael Chapel remained, as he does at the time of this writing, incarcerated for crimes that he did not and could not have committed.

Justice denied.

Epilogue

When I first contacted Christopher Routh – the former fourteen-year-old boy laid on the tracks of the *Gwinnett County Railroad* in 2001, I told him that a fitting end to this book would be for him to ride back into Gwinnett County on his big white horse and defeat Danny Porter once more. It would be for a just cause – freedom for Michael Chapel. He could then ride off into the sunset – a conquering hero.

After being falsely accused of rape and murder by GCPD and Danny Porter as a child, Routh weathered an unimaginable storm. Thanks to the unwavering support of his family and a small group of their friends, spearheaded by Christopher's unflappable and unrelenting father, Charlie, who worked relentlessly to bring the truth to light. The boy was fully exonerated. In typical fashion, Porter refused to admit defeat, even when the judge and jury settled it.

According to his father, Charlie, Christopher Routh went to jail as a boy but returned home from his lengthy incarceration, a man – much wiser and more experienced than his diminutive number of years would indicate.

Routh became a death-qualified public defender and has dedicated his life to defending those who cannot defend themselves. He learned the Gwinnett County Justice System as well as the *Gwinnett County Railroad* firsthand. What Routh told me is the truth of the matter. When boiled down to its essence, the justice system has failed Michael Chapel, and that cannot be undone.

What can be done is that you and I climb up on our white horses and ride to his rescue. We can be the conquering heroes. We must ride our horses and raise our voices. We must let people know that a true American Hero is languishing in a prison cell in South Georgia – a political prisoner for twenty-eight years at the time of this writing. He is incarcerated by lies, mistruths, misdeeds, and every machination of the devils that ruled Gwinnett County for the better part of the last three decades.

Danny Porter's successor, Patsy Austin-Gatson announced the formation of the Convictions Integrity Unit on Thursday, April 15, 2021, twenty-eight years to the day of Emogene Thompson's murder. Austin-Gatson intends to look at past convictions in Gwinnett County to ensure the integrity of those convictions.

Michael Chapel

This action by the new District Attorney breathed life into the Michael Chapel is Innocent Project, and hundreds of volunteers began to send emails and letters to Madame District Attorney calling on her to reopen the Chapel case.

Shortly after the announcement of the Convictions Integrity Unit, the State Bar of Georgia announced a rule change that will allow for sanctions, including disbarment for prosecutors who hide evidence and otherwise violate the civil rights of defendants.

The State Bar's action, as well as the actions of the new Gwinnett County District Attorney, fall into a pattern of measures currently being taken around the country in an effort to refine and reform our judicial system that has allowed it to be alarmingly more common for an innocent person to be convicted, and nearly impossible for an innocent person to overturn that wrongful conviction.

Michael Chapel has exhausted his appeals process in futility. He has afforded himself every option at his disposal in order to prove his innocence to the courts. They have, at all levels, refused to listen.

We are Michael Chapel's only hope. Michael Chapel will only have justice when enough of us raise our collective voices. Write to the new DA, our congresspersons, the attorney general, the governor, the president, the judges, the parole board, the chief of police, police unions, and everyone willing or able to help. Call, write, email, SCREAM!

We must force the system to re-examine this case. Michael Chapel has declared for twenty-eight years, "I'm telling the truth, and the truth isn't working."

It is time for the truth to have its day. I have reviewed close to twenty thousand documents in this case and read the witness statements. I have studied the evidence, uncovered new evidence, interviewed witnesses, spoke to former investigators, former attorneys, and many people associated with the case.

I have reviewed, organized, and duplicated the investigative files of Phil Sullivan, Dennis Miller, Boris Korczak, Pamela Holcombe, Edward Han-

Epilogue

son, and many others.

What I am willing to declare as a result of all these investigations, what is clear from an overwhelming cache of evidence is that Michael Harold Chapel was not at the Gwinnco Muffler Shop on April 15, 1993, from the hours of 2030 at least until after shift change at 2245. He could not be the perpetrator of the heinous crime that occurred at that place at or around 2200 according to the Medical Examiner's window of death and the time the victim arrived at the scene.

It is now irrefutable that there were dirty cops throughout the rank and file of GCPD, just as Chapel declared in 1993 when he alleged that the bad guys were framing him in order for them to take him off the street. He contended that his street-level investigations into those rank-and-file dirty cops were beginning to make them uncomfortable.

What Chapel did not know then was how high up the rank and file the corruption rose. We can confirm that it rose to the very top as members of the GCPD leadership participated in both the planning of the illegal manufacturing of the case against Chapel and the active cover-up that took place in connection with the suicide of J. P. Morgan and the subsequent destruction of evidence that occurred at that scene.

We also have evidence that members of the District Attorney's team suborned perjury, coerced, and threatened witnesses, first responders, and civilian employees. The truth of this case is now and has always been that Michael Harold Chapel was a threat to various members of the GCPD and Gwinnett County's judicial system.

Emogene Thompson's murder offered them a canvas, so they framed the portrait. For this frame job to work, they had to let another group of two-bit hustlers and thugs, along with some dirty cops, literally get away with murder, and that is precisely what they did.

Re-Enactment

Some direct quotes are not available. The timeline and location is based on the records; while conversations are based upon a preponderance of the evidence and are dramatized for publication.

Thursday, April 15, 1993. Sugar Hill, Georgia.

8:30 PM: Emogene Thompson finishes dinner with her son, Michael Thompson, at a local Waffle House. Emogene Thompson returns home. Michael Thompson returns to Amy Parker's trailer.

8:30 PM: Officer Michael Chapel, Officer Brian Reddy, Sergeant D.E. Stone arrive at Firehouse 14 on Buford Highway.

8:45 PM: A police officer appears at Gwinnco Muffler Shop, apparently watching traffic. Caucasian man, white shirt, white boxy car.

9:30 PM: The police officer remains at Gwinnco, apparently watching traffic. Caucasian man, white shirt, white boxy car.

9:30 PM: Michael Thompson leaves Amy Parker's trailer *"to go get something to eat."*

9:45 PM: Amy Parker goes next door to Emogene Thompson's trailer to "use the phone." No phone calls in or out in that time frame, according to phone records. Parker was last seen near Emogene Thompson's vehicle. The tire was slashed before Emogene Thompson's departure for work.

"If somebody wanted to stick the tire..."

Amy Parker

#michaelchapelisinnnocent

9:50 PM: Emogene Thompson leaves for work at her normal time.

9:55 PM: David McGaha sees Emogene Thompson's vehicle at Gwinnco. No other vehicles. (Gwinnco Muffler Shop is 1.7 miles from Thompson's Driveway.)

9:56 PM: Officer Chapel receives a radio call from Gwinnett County Police Dispatch.

Michael Chapel at Firehouse #14 at the time of the murder

The Police radio recordings confirming Chapel's alibi were "lost."

#michaelchapelisinnocent

< 10:00 PM: Officer Chapel leaves Firehouse 14 en route to the assigned call at Arden Road. (Opposite direction of Gwinco Muffler.)

< 10:00 PM: Ron Flashner sees a vehicle that uniquely matches the description of Michael Thompson's vehicle backed up (trunk to trunk) at Gwinnco, with three or four individuals around the victim's vehicle.

Witnesses saw three or four figures through heavy engine smoke.

The victim's son owned a car matching the smoking vehicle.

#michaelchapelisinnocent

10:00 PM: End of Window of death provided by the M. E. (9:00 PM – 10:00 PM)

> 10:00 PM: Officer Brian Reddy leaves Firehouse 14, *"heading North up Buford Highway."*

> 10 PM: Blue Light activity, an officer described as six-foot, medium build.

What the witnesses saw...

"Six foot, medium build"

10:11 PM: Officer Chapel arrives at Arden Road assignment, stays about 10 minutes, *"courteous and nice."*

10:17 PM: Sergeant Stones used precinct phone to call home, *"20 minutes after Chapel left Firehouse."*

< 10:30 PM: Michael Thompson returns to Amy Parker with a *"Subway cup of ice and some brownies."* Thompson watches a few minutes of the Simpsons and leaves to *"go check on a job."*

10:30 PM: Michael Thompson returns from job search, goes home shortly after that. Neighbors do not *"hear"* him leave again.

10:30 PM: Michael Chapel returns to the precinct, end of watch.

10:45 PM: Michael Chapel leaves precinct, goes home to family.

11:00 PM: Michael Thompson pages drug dealer in Hiawassee, Georgia.

Midnight: Small sedan with a busted taillight seen at Gwinnco, behind victim's vehicle.

Testimony would later tell us that J. P. Morgan used Michael Thompson as a 'do boy' in his nefarious dealings with the local drug traffickers. Morgan was accused of as much at the Hall County jail when Walt Britt fingered him as the scheme's mastermind to frame Chapel. Instead of answering these accusations, Morgan took the coward's way out and discharged his service weapon into his right temple.

We also know that the District Attorney's office had reason to believe that Thompson's associate, Dennis Shelton was at the scene. Thompson, Shelton, and at least one other person are believed to have arrived at the scene, as described by Ron Flashner, shortly before 10:00 PM and just moments after Emogene Thompson had turned into the muffler shop out of desperation with a flat tire.

Emogene Thompson had just lit a cigarette, taken from a new pack in her cigarette case, as a familiar 'big car' began backing into the muffler shop behind her. She must have felt relieved as she turned the ignition switch to the on position to lower her window.

'My sweet son Mikey just happened by and noticed my plight,' she may have thought to herself.

"Bless you boys!" she might have said as one of the men went past her now partially open window to "examine" the flat tire.

Shelton already had a hand on the passenger door handle when Mikey calls out from the driver's side of his car as he is approaching the vehicle, "let us in, Mom, it's raining something fierce."

Emogene places the lit cigarette in the ashtray, unlocks the doors, and wonders why Dennis Shelton was climbing into her front passenger seat with a long stem yellow rose, which he places on the dash. "For you, Mrs. T."

Mikey climbs in behind Shelton, sipping from a Subway drinking cup, and the trigger man climbs in behind Emogene Thompson.

"Where is your purse, Mom?" Mikey asks flatly, noting that his mother is carrying her necessaries in her cigarette case and a plastic baggie on the front seat.

Re-Enactment

Startled, Emogene asks, "Why do you need to know where my purse is, Son?"

"The money, Mom, I'm gonna need the money."

"Well, it's not here, and you boys can just go on home now!" Ms. Thompson starts to turn her head toward her son. The first bullet entered her neck just below her left ear and exited the extreme right of her right eye socket. It nicked the windshield after it passed through and destroyed the victim's eyeglasses leaving them broken and bloody laying on the center hump under the console.

The assailant then reaches his left arm around the headrest of the driver's seat, places the barrel of the .38 on the back of the victim's down-angled head, and fires the second shot. Shelton begins to exit the vehicle between shots, allowing several droplets of blood to be deposited inside the passenger door well.

All three men in the vehicle have absorbed at least a portion of the high-velocity blood spatter that forensic scientists say should have been present in the vehicle under the circumstances. The lid from Thompson's Subway cup is deposited on the back floorboard and abandoned to the scene.

The men did a cursory search for the purse in the dark and quickly decided to exit the scene. Upon exiting the vehicle from the driver's rear, the shooter then reached in through the partially open window and deployed the automatic door locks. All three men dripped blood onto the asphalt outside the vehicle on both sides. The rain washed away some but not all of the blood.

Within ten minutes of the big, smoking sedan exiting the muffler shop, the spare patrol car is back on the scene with blue lights on. A police officer in full rain gear, complete with smokie hat rain cover, is seen walking up to the victim's vehicle with a flashlight in his hand. By the time Kautter and Omodt pass the muffler shop, the blue lights are off, and the six-foot cop is standing next to the driver's door.

Most of the patrol officers of GCPD carried crime scene kits in their vehicles, which would have allowed an experienced officer to reach through the partially open window, swab fresh blood from the victim, and hermetically seal the swab stick for later use.

Within seconds of them passing the muffler shop, a second police car begins to catch and overtake Kautter and Omodt. They were both inebriated and likely nervous with the presence of law enforcement.

It is not known who this second officer was, though Officer Brian Reddy had been gone from the firehouse for five to ten minutes by now. Reddy was last seen by Sergeant Stone *"heading north up Buford Highway,"* the same direction of the muffler shop, but he logged himself at a convenience store about a mile from the scene.

Reddy also fit the general description of Chapel, same build, hairstyle, facial hair, and general look – such that they were often accused of being brothers, though Latty claimed Chapel was a more handsome fellow. It is unknown why Reddy was not included in the pictorial lineup.

By 8:30 AM: April 16, the A Shift at Firehouse 14 relieved the C Shift. A Shift responded to the scene where Emogene Thompson's body was found.

Shortly after their arrival on the scene, GCPD began to arrive, as did Michael Thompson, acting strange according to at least one firefighter. Thompson seemed to be aware of his mother's demise, despite being held away from the vehicle, and according to the firefighter, he demonstrably faked crying, as *"there wasn't a tear in his eye"* when he removed his hands from his face.

Thompson immediately began to question detectives at the scene, not about his mother's condition or how she met her demise. He asked only the whereabouts of his mother's purse.

Thompson would go on to collect $115,000.00 in life insurance money from his mother's policy. He spent the bulk of this money on a Corvette, crack cocaine, and a cruise with Amy Parker. By the time Chapel's trial rolled around, Thompson was again broke, had been arrested several times for financial fraud, and was unable to pay for his mother's funeral.

Thompson was heard by at least a dozen people saying that Michael Chapel did not murder his mother, but he needed Chapel to be convicted of the crime so he could collect millions from Gwinnett County.

Re-Enactment

A review of the facts surrounding Tax Day, April 15, 1993, leaves no question that at least one rogue Gwinnett County Police officer worked with a small group of local thugs and drug dealers. Together, they plotted the murder of Emogene Thompson and the subsequent framing of officer Chapel for that crime.

By the time investigators and the District Attorney realized they had been duped, they had all gone too far and refused to admit their mistake. A criminal conspiracy and corrupt cabal were born in Gwinnett County that reached all the way to the top of the Police Department and the District Attorney's Office.

The *Gwinnett County Railroad* would run over Michael Chapel, Christopher Routh, Quintrellis Head, and countless others.

Michael Chapel has paid an unimaginable price for doing his job, while most of the self-serving men responsible for the unconscionable crimes against him have prospered. Though they have prospered, they have not escaped. There is no statute of limitations for murder, accessory to murder, or conspiracy involving murder.

The truth is coming, it will be known, and Lady Justice will have her day.

Fiat Justitia ruat Caelum.

Evidence referred to in this book including case records, trial transcripts, investogators notes, crime scene photos, videos, and other relevant documentation can be reviewed at www.michaelchapel.com

The Michael Chapel is Innocent Project

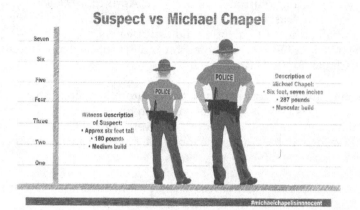

Suspect vs Michael Chapel

Seven
Six
Five
Four
Three
Two
One

Witness Description
of Suspect:
• Approx six feet tall
• 180 pounds
• Medium build

POLICE
POLICE

Description of
Michael Chapel:
• Six feet, seven inches
• 287 pounds
• Muscular build

#michaelchapelisinnnocent

Join the fight to free Michael Chapel and bring the truth to light.
www.michaelchapel.com
www.facebook.com/groups/891026941742657

Please write to:

Gwinnett County District Attorney:
Patsy Austin-Gatson
Gwinnett Justice & Administration Center
75 Langley Drive
Lawrenceville, GA 30046

770-822-8000
patsy.austin-gatson@gwinnettcounty.com
Convictions Integrity Unit
daciu@gwinnettcounty.com

To Parole Board Members:
State Board of Pardons and Paroles
2 Martin Luther King Drive SE
PO Box 70
Atlanta, GA 30334
Ludowici, GA 31316

Re: Michael Harold Chapel #845840
Long Unit

Governor:
Office of the Governor Brian Kemp
206 Washington Street
Suite 203, State Capitol
Atlanta, GA 30334

404-656-1776
gov.georgia.gov

Attorney General:
Office of the Attorney General Chris Carr
40 Capitol Square, SW
Atlanta, GA 30334

404-458-3600
law.georgia.gov

Police Chief:
Gwinnett County Police Chief Brett West
75 Langley Drive
Lawrenceville, GA 30046

770-513-5000
Brett.West@gwinnettcounty.com

Police Union:
Police Benevolent Association (PBA)
Joseph Naia (Georgia Division)

800-233-3506

President:
The Office of the President of the United States Joseph R. Biden
1600 Pennsylvania Avenue NW
Washington, DC 20500

About the Authors

Henry Ball – Executive, Author, the Daddy-O as he's known at home first arrived in the thriving metropolis of – *Hotlanta* – where he fell into an Atlanta Braves cap but maintained his purple and gold bloodline as a die-hard LSU Tiger fan. Henry's fearlessness and entrepreneurial spirit opened the door of opportunity – first one and then another; with courage and determination, Henry finds success in hard work.

Henry's award-winning debut novel, Sister of Sorrows, was published in December 2020. Instead of reveling in success, Henry accepted the next challenge before the ink dried. Henry heard the exit interview of Danny Porter, aired on Atlanta's WSB Radio following Porter's 2020 defeat in the Gwinnett County District Attorney's race.

Porter described the Chapel case as one that best defined his tenure as chief prosecutor. Henry knew from years of research that Michael Chapel is Innocent and Porter's arrogance in boasting about such an injustice incensed the newly published author, inspiring this book.

Henry has reviewed thousands of documents, read the witness statements, spoken to witnesses, studied the evidence, uncovered new evidence and exposed the manufactured case against Michael Harold Chapel.

Deborah Ann Dahlmann – Editor-in-Chief of Storied Press, LLC is also Henry Ball's eldest sister. Deborah and her young family moved to Gwinnett County, Georgia during the construction boom in 1984. Here is where she raised two children, Michael and Miechelle Elizabeth Bourgeois.

Deborah secured employment with a Fortune 500 Real Estate Investment Firm and for the next eight years served as a project manager. She was at the office the day the verdict against Michael Chapel was handed down, her heart broke for her dear friends, Michael and Eren Chapel.

Deborah led a team of volunteers, including some of her co-workers, together with Eren Chapel, they spread the word far and as wide. Deborah experienced firsthand, the intimidation tactics employed by the Gwinnett County authorities who wielded threats of arrest if they did not cease and desist in their defense of Michael Chapel.

Although life and business have taken Deborah away from Gwinnett, first to Florida and then Washington State, Deborah has not wavered from her belief in Michael Chapel's innocence. When she took the call in November 2020 from her "little" brother Henry asking her to assist with the Chapel project, she showed no fear, no hesitation. Let's do it!